WEDDING PLANNER

*A step by step guide
to your special day*

ELIZABETH CATHERINE MYERS

how to books

Published by How To Books Ltd,
Spring Hill House, Spring Hill Road, Begbroke
Oxford OX5 1RX. United Kingdom
Tel: (01865) 375794. Fax: (01865) 379162
info@howtobooks.co.uk
www.howtobooks.co.uk

How To Books greatly reduce the carbon footprint of their books by sourcing their
typesetting and printing in the UK.

British Library Cataloguing in Publication Data.
A catalogue record for this book is available from the British Library.

ISBN 978 1 84528 235 6

Produced for How To Books by Deer Park Productions, Tavistock, Devon
Typeset by Baseline Arts Ltd, Oxford
Printed and bound by Cromwell Press Ltd, Trowbridge, Wiltshire

NOTE: The material contained in this book is set out in good faith for general guidance and
no liability can be accepted for loss or expense incurred as a result of relying in particular
circumstances on statements made in this book. The laws and regulations are complex and
liable to change, and readers should check the current position with the relevant
authorities before making personal arrangements.

CONTENTS

INTRODUCTION

Congratulations! You have announced your engagement and it should be one of the happiest times of your life.

This book has been written to try to help you keep the feeling of being on top of the world by getting you through all the areas you need to plan for your wedding and reception.

There is space to write in the book so you can then keep it as a souvenir of your wedding plans.

This book is a result of many years of working in event management, but it also benefits from a personal touch because it has been written alongside planning my own wedding.

I hope the chapters in this book help you to organise and plan all the areas of your wedding and reception so that you can enjoy the build up to your wedding day without feeling too stressed.

Good luck and remember to enjoy this time in your life as it will pass very quickly!

INTRODUCING THE BRIDE AND GROOM

	Bride	**Groom**
Name:		
Date of birth:		
Place of birth:		

Date we met:

Place we met:

What happened:

Date we got engaged:

Place we got engaged:

What happened:

GETTING STARTED

Once you have had time to celebrate your engagement and enjoy the moment, it can often be very daunting knowing where to start with planning your wedding and reception.

The key to successful planning is to break everything down into small manageable tasks which are easy to complete. If you can easily tick things off your checklist as you do them it will make you feel as though you are making progress, and by taking small steps you can easily accomplish all the big tasks that go with organising your wedding.

There are a few things to keep in mind when you start planning your wedding:

◆ The earlier you start planning the better. Looking for the best options for your venue, food, car, cake, photographer, DJ and everything else will be time consuming. If you leave it late it will put more pressure on you as well as potentially missing out on the best deal.

◆ Take out wedding insurance at an early stage for cover required. Even with the most detailed planning, it is still possible for something to happen which could prevent the wedding day going ahead. What if the Groom gets food poisoning the night before? What if the venue gets flooded a few days before your reception? Insurance will not help to cope with the stress or the upset of having to postpone a wedding but at least it will provide financial compensation.

◆ Make sure you agree everything with your suppliers **in writing**. If you (and the supplier) have all the details written down there is less scope for a mistake to be made. Ensure the correct wedding date is written down. Check the services/items to be provided are described clearly and a price is agreed. If there are optional services, make sure these are listed separately and any additional costs for these are clearly defined. Make sure you clarify when deposits and further instalments are due and the amount you need to pay. You may also want to ask for references from previous clients.

◆ Always check with each supplier what their back up plan is in case something goes wrong beyond their control.

◆ Once you have made a booking, keep checking at regular intervals that everything is in order. Ring around every supplier you have booked a few days before your wedding for a final check.

◆ Try to keep some evenings and weekends 'wedding free' in the run up to your wedding where you and your partner talk about other things and spend time together doing something you both enjoy. Have a soak in the bath, go out for a walk or go to the cinema but ban all talk of menu choices, florists and dress fittings.

Finally, the lead up to your wedding can be very exciting but it can also be very stressful. It is very easy to lose sight of why you are having the wedding in the first place. Thorough planning is important to ensure your wedding goes as you want it to, but if something unexpected does happen, try to see the funny side and don't let it spoil your big day.

BUDGET PLANNER

In order to keep your spending within budget you will need to work out how much you can afford for each part of your wedding reception and stick to that budget or better still, try to spend less.

If you make a detailed list of all the things you require for your wedding reception, you can break the budget down which will make it easier for you to manage your spending. If you are able to, include a contingency budget for unexpected items.

In future chapters, there is information about who is traditionally responsible for paying for different areas of the wedding and reception. However, in current times there tends to be no set format regarding who covers the cost. It all depends on each couple and their particular circumstances. It is advisable to sit down at the outset with anyone who may be involved in the wedding finances. You can then clarify what they can afford to pay for and what is their financial limit. It is also polite to consult them over your choices for any particular items they are paying for so they are kept informed of your plans and feel as though they are having an input.

Here is a list of items you may need to budget for to get you started but there are spaces to add extra items which you may want to include:

Item	Budget	Actual Cost	Paid for by
Invitations			
Postage			
Bride's dress			
Bridesmaids' dresses			
Bride's shoes			
Accessories/Hair/Make-up			
Wedding rings			
Groom's attire			
Best man/ushers' attire			
Church/Civil Ceremony/ Register Office			
Order of Service			
Reception Venue Hire			
Catering – Day reception			
Catering – Evening			
Drinks Reception			
Drinks for Toast			
Wedding Cake			
Music/Entertainment			

Item	Budget	Actual Cost	Paid for by
Flowers			
Decorations including favours /place cards/menus			
Transport:			
Bride to wedding service			
Bridesmaids to wedding service			
Groom to wedding service			
Bride & Groom to reception			
Bride & Groom away from reception			
Photographer			
Videographer			
Wedding night accommodation for Bride/Groom			
Honeymoon			
Insurance			
Contingency			
Total			

CHAPTER 1

THE MAIN CHARACTERS

THE BRIDE

The responsibilities of the Bride are:

◆ **To be the centre of attention and the star of the show**
During the planning stages of the wedding, the Bride will be reminded countless times that it is her day and her chance to be centre of attention in front of all her family and friends.

For some brides, who are perhaps more reserved, this could be a very daunting prospect so it is worth thinking about how to cope with the attention and how you will feel on the day.

If it is something that makes you feel anxious, it may be worth investigating relaxation techniques to help with any nerves.

◆ **Organising the wedding day**
The Bride is responsible for the overall planning and organisation of the day. There will be a lot of details to consider and arrangements to make.

Although wedding planning can be stressful at times, there are many techniques that can be used to help make your life easier in the run up to the wedding. By breaking down each area that you need to plan into small tasks, it will make it easier to get things done on your list and tick them off which will make you feel as though you are making progress. The checklists in this book are designed to help you to keep track of everything you need to do but you may want to add your own tasks to them.

If you are writing your own 'to do' lists alongside these, consider the following:

As an example, if one of your tasks is 'Make the wedding favours', this could be broken down into steps as follows:-

❖ *Browse internet for ideas for small boxes/bags*
❖ *Choose boxes/bags and place order for correct amount (allow for a few extra)*
❖ *Browse internet for ideas for chocolates/sweets for the favours*
❖ *Choose favourite and place order for correct amount (allow for a few extra)*
❖ *Browse shops for suitable ribbon*
❖ *Work out quantity of ribbon needed and place order*
❖ *Assemble wedding favours*

By breaking the task down into steps, each sub-task is more easily achievable.

In addition to the use of checklists, remember, you are not doing this alone. Your Groom, your bridesmaids and members of your family may all be willing to

help out so if you can delegate some of the tasks to people you trust and who are responsible, you won't feel that you have to do everything yourself.

However, whilst family members may want to help, sometimes this can feel a little overwhelming for the Bride, who has a very fine line to tread to plan the day of her dreams at the same time as making sure both families feel involved, as well as not offending members of either family with any decisions that she makes.

◆ **Planning the budget and how to pay for the day**
Talking about finances can be awkward but if you can tackle this at the outset, it will make the planning and organisation easier. Once you know how much money you have to spend and who will be contributing to the cost of the wedding, you can then decide what you will spend the money on.

Traditionally, the Bride's father paid for the wedding reception and the Groom would pay for certain items but in more recent times many couples are opting to pay for their wedding themselves. This may give them more freedom to make decisions on how to spend the money and perhaps to organise things in the way they want to rather than having to consider other people's preferences.

If the cost of the wedding is being funded by members of the Bride and Groom's families (as well as the couple themselves), it is polite to consult with the funders over the items they are paying for to ensure they are happy.

◆ **Making decisions on all aspects of the day**
The Bride has the responsibility of making all the decisions for every aspect of the wedding day such as:

❖ Ceremony	❖ Flowers
❖ Reception Venue	❖ Cars
❖ Catering	❖ Rings
❖ Cake	❖ Invitations
❖ Photographer	❖ Gift Lists
❖ Videographer	❖ First Dance

Many couples decide to make joint decisions as the day is for both of them.

◆ **Choosing the wedding dress**
Depending on your budget this could be the most expensive item of clothing the Bride has ever bought. See section on page 100.

◆ **To choose bridesmaids and their outfits**
The Bride needs to decide how many bridesmaids she is going to have (if any) and what they are going to wear.

Her matron of honour or Chief Bridesmaid will need to have the following qualities:

❖ *To be supportive*
❖ *To be enthusiastic about the wedding*
❖ *To be calm at all times*
❖ *To be reliable*
❖ *To be punctual*
❖ *To be responsible*
❖ *To carry out the tasks the Bride has asked her to the best of her ability.*

The Bride's father traditionally pays for the Bridesmaids' outfits. However, the Bride and Groom or even the Bridesmaids may be happy to pay for the outfits themselves. It is important to clarify who will be responsible for payment at the outset to ensure they can afford to do so and are happy to do so.

◆ **Selecting gifts for the female attendants**
As the bridesmaids will do a wonderful job of supporting the Bride on her big day, the Bride is responsible for selecting suitable gifts as a thank you to all her assistants on the day.

Her bridesmaids should all be people the Bride knows well and therefore selecting something personal would be appropriate as well as perhaps something that will be a keepsake of the day.

◆ **Attending wedding rehearsal**
The Bride should attend the wedding rehearsal along with other key members of

the wedding party. The wedding rehearsal enables all the main participants in the ceremony to run through what will happen and at which points during the ceremony they will need to perform their duties.

◆ **Taking part in the line up at the reception**
It is traditional for all the members of the wedding party to greet all the guests as they file into the reception. This gives the Bride and Groom the opportunity to welcome every guest to their reception and gives each guest the opportunity to say a few words to the Bride and Groom.

◆ **Giving out thank you gifts during Groom's speech**
Part of the Groom's responsibility is to thank all the members of the wedding party and at this point the Bride hands out the gifts that she and the Groom have selected.

It has become more common for the Bride to give a speech too. In some cases, the Bride feels she would like to say a few words rather than having the Groom do all the talking. This is personal preference but something for consideration.

◆ **Writing the thank you cards**
The responsibility of the thank you cards again is traditionally the responsibility of the Bride but modern couples may decide to make a joint effort with this task. It is likely that both the Bride and Groom will have different writing styles so this would help to vary the responses written in the cards.

THE CHIEF BRIDESMAID OR MATRON OF HONOUR

The responsibilities of the Chief Bridesmaid are:

◆ **Helping the Bride choose her dress**
Choosing the right dress is probably going to be a big decision for the Bride, so having her Chief Bridesmaid there for support and approval is likely to be very important to her.

The Bride is going to need someone she can trust to help her make the right decision, so she will need an honest opinion as to which dress is the correct choice. The Chief Bridesmaid will also need to ensure she is advising with the best interest of the Bride at heart and is not being influenced by her own personal preferences.

◆ **Helping to choose Bridesmaids' dresses**
The Chief Bridesmaid has a vested interest in helping with the choice of bridesmaids' dresses as she will have to wear what the Bride decides upon. It is important that the Chief Bridesmaid consults with the Bride over colour and style as the bridal party need to look their best – without upstaging the Bride, of course!.

◆ **Organising the hen party**
It is traditional for the Chief
Bridesmaid to organise the hen party
for the Bride. However, the Bride may
decide to take on this responsibility
herself. See chapter on hen parties on
page 186.

◆ **Helping with last minute preparations**
If needed, the Chief Bridesmaid should
be available the day before and on the
morning of the wedding to help with
last minute preparations and to run
errands to ensure everything is in place
for the ceremony and reception.

◆ **Looking after other bridesmaids and
ensuring they do what they've been
asked**
The Chief Bridesmaid needs to brief
the other bridesmaids, flower girl and
page boys on any tasks they have been
asked to carry out. She is also
responsible for looking after them
(especially the younger ones) on the
way to the ceremony and during the
ceremony.

◆ **Assisting the Bride to get ready before the wedding**
As the Bride prepares for the wedding, the Chief Bridesmaid should be there to assist and keep the Bride calm. In particular, skills with hair and make up are useful in case something does not go to plan.

◆ **Assisting the Bride during the day**
It is the role of the Chief Bridesmaid to help the Bride on the day. This includes adjusting her veil and train of her dress on arrival at the ceremony and holding her bouquet during the ceremony. If the Bride prepares a bag of essential items (see page 118), the Chief Bridesmaid should ensure this is kept somewhere within easy access. Her duties could even extend as far as accompanying the Bride to the bathroom, if the Bride's dress is particularly large or awkward to handle.

◆ **Taking part in the line up**
As part of the bridal party, the Chief Bridesmaid should also take part in the line up and greet all the guests as they enter the reception room. This gives her the opportunity to meet all the guests in person.

If there are other bridesmaids too, their duties involve helping the Chief Bridesmaid to ensure the day runs smoothly as well as attending dress fittings and the hen party (if they are old enough) before the wedding.

Some Brides choose to have a very young bridesmaid or flower girl to scatter petals down the aisle at the start of the wedding procession or to carry a basket of flowers.

They may also want young pageboys in the procession or a young ring bearer.

INSTRUCTIONS FOR THE CHIEF BRIDESMAID

Although the Chief Bridesmaid may be around during all the preparations and will be briefed by the Bride as to what she needs to do on the day, it may be useful to prepare a written briefing for the Chief Bridesmaid with tasks and telephone numbers of key people. She will be able to keep this with her on the day so she has access to important information if necessary.

The briefing can only be prepared a few weeks before the wedding as you will need to include details of the suppliers and timings on the day, but if you keep this in mind at the start of your plans you can keep a note of things you might want to include.

The instructions could be along the lines of:

Dear

Thank you for agreeing to be my Chief Bridesmaid on 3rd November 20xx.

Although we have already talked about what you need to do on the day, we thought it would be useful to give you some information in writing to help you on the day.

1. We will need you to go to the florist on the morning of the wedding and pick up the bouquets. The florist is at 15 High Street, Littletown. Tel: XXXX XXXXXX

2. Please can you be at Liz's parents' house by midday. This will give enough time for the hairdresser and make-up person to transform us.

3. You will be leaving in the second car from the house at 2.30pm with the younger Bridesmaids.

4. Please take the bag of Liz's essential items with you. This can be left in the car during the wedding ceremony but please remember to take this into the reception venue and leave it in Liz's room so she can access it if necessary.

5. When you arrive at the reception venue, please can you check that the cake has been assembled with the flowers on each tier. Please can you also make sure the venue staff have lit all the candles.

Useful telephone numbers that you might need:

Jonathan	XXXX XXXX XXXX
Liz	XXXX XXXX XXXX
Reception Venue	XXXX XXXX XXXX

Thank you for agreeing to help us with our wedding ceremony.

We are looking forward to a wonderful day.

Best wishes,

Liz and Jonathan

MOTHER OF THE BRIDE

The responsibilities of the Mother of the Bride (MOTB) are:

◆ **Helping the Bride to plan her day**
The MOTB should be there to provide help and advice (when requested) whilst respecting the Bride's ideas and wishes.

◆ **Helping the Bride to select her dress**
The MOTB may also be involved in the decision regarding the Bride's dress. However, she should consider the Bride's taste in clothing and should not try to influence the Bride if her taste is different.

◆ **Assisting with putting the guest list together**
The Bride may need some assistance with putting the guest list together, so the MOTB is well placed to give advice on people to invite from the Bride's side of the family as well as friends of the Bride's mother and father. Family politics may come into play so the MOTB can help to ensure the Bride does not have additional stress from family members.

◆ **Helping with setting the budget**
As it is traditional for the parents of the Bride to pay for the reception, the MOTB can assist with the initial budgeting for the wedding. However, it is important at the early stages that

the parents of the Bride outline clearly what they are willing to pay for so there are no misunderstandings when it comes to paying the suppliers.

◆ **Choosing her own outfit for the wedding**

As an important member of the wedding party who will also be on show all day, the MOTB's outfit needs to be carefully chosen with the help of the Bride. At the same time, the MOTB should liaise with the Groom's mother to ensure outfits do not clash or even worse, that they do not both turn up wearing the same outfit!

◆ **Assisting with hotel arrangements for out of town guests**

If guests are coming from further afield, the MOTB can help the Bride by assisting the guests with arrangements for overnight accommodation. However, if the Bride and Groom do not feel this is necessary, they can include accommodation information with their invitations so that guests can easily book their own accommodation.

◆ **Assist the Bride with seating plans for the reception**
Seating plans for the wedding reception can be a minefield if certain personalities clash. The MOTB should have enough knowledge of the Bride's family and her own guests to be able to help the Bride arrange a suitable seating plan. The Groom and the Groom's mother may need to be consulted too in order to offer advice on the Groom's family and friends of the Groom's parents.

◆ **Look after the guests on the day**
Although the day ultimately belongs to the Bride and Groom, it will be very hectic for them and there will be a limit to how much time they will have to spend with their guests. The MOTB is therefore also responsible for circulating amongst the guests and ensuring they are enjoying the day.

◆ **Standing in the line up**
The MOTB is also part of the line up to greet guests when they enter the reception room.

MOTHER OF THE GROOM

The responsibilities of the mother of the Groom (MOTG) are:

◆ **Assisting with putting the guest list together**
The MOTG can offer advice on creating the guest list for the
Groom's family as well as the guests that she and the Groom's
father would like to invite.

◆ **Liaising with the MOTB over outfits**
The MOTG needs to liaise with the MOTB to ensure their outfits
complement each other.

◆ **Assisting with hotel arrangements for out of town guests**
In the same way the MOTB may take responsibility for helping
her out of town guests with booking accommodation, the
MOTG can take responsibility for the same task for her guests.
However, this should be discussed with the Bride and Groom
and with the MOTB to ensure everyone is happy and has a clear
understanding over who is responsible for which guests.

◆ **Standing in the line up**
The MOTG is also part of the line up to greet guests when they
enter the reception room.

THE GROOM

The responsibilities of the Groom are:

◆ **Booking the ceremony**
It is traditional for the Groom to make the arrangements for booking the ceremony and to ensure all the correct paperwork/information is submitted to the person conducting the ceremony. However, in more recent times, the Bride and Groom often take joint responsibility for this task which makes sense if the Bride is planning the overall day.

◆ **Selecting the Best Man and ushers**
The Groom needs to decide on who should be his Best Man and how many ushers he is going to have as well as choosing what they are going to wear.

Being the Best Man is a responsible role, so whoever the groom chooses will need to be:
❖ *Supportive*
❖ *Calm at all times*
❖ *Reliable*
❖ *Punctual*
❖ *and prepared to accept the responsibility of carrying out the tasks the Groom has asked him to, to the best of his ability.*

◆ **Deciding what the male members of the wedding party will wear**
Traditionally, the Groom pays for the suit hire of the male
attendants but they may be happy to pay for their own suit
hire. However, it is advisable to discuss this with them at the
outset to ensure they are willing to bear the cost, especially if
they are likely to be costly.

◆ **Buying the wedding ring(s)**
It is traditional for the Groom to buy
the Bride's wedding ring and for the
Bride to buy the Groom's ring. However,
modern couples often choose the rings
together and pay for them jointly.

◆ **Buying gifts for the male members of
the wedding party**
As a thank you for all their support before and on the wedding
day, the Groom is responsible for choosing gifts for all the male
attendants, such as the Best Man, Ushers and Father of the
Bride and Groom.

Gifts should be personal and if possible should be a keepsake of
the day.

The Groom may also want to buy flowers for his mother and
the Bride's mother to thank them for their support.

◆ **Planning the honeymoon**

Another tradition is for the Groom to plan the honeymoon as a surprise. However, once again, modern couples may decide to choose and pay for the honeymoon themselves.

If the Groom does decide to keep the destination a secret, it is a good idea to advise the Bride of the type of climate she can expect so that she can pack the appropriate clothing for the trip.

◆ **Arranging transport**

Again, tradition dictates that the Groom is responsible for his own transport arrangements to the wedding and then for himself and his bride to the reception but this could end up as another shared task and cost between the Bride and Groom.

As well as modes of transport, it is useful to plan how each member of the wedding party will get to the ceremony and then to the reception and finally home again afterwards.

◆ **Attending wedding rehearsal**

The Groom should attend the wedding rehearsal along with other key members of the wedding party. The wedding rehearsal enables all the main participants in the ceremony to run through what will happen and at which points during the ceremony they will need to perform their duties.

◆ **Taking part in the line up at the reception**
It is traditional for all the members of the wedding party to greet all the guests as they file into the reception. This gives the Bride and Groom the opportunity to welcome every guest to their reception and gives each guest the opportunity to say a few words to the Bride and Groom.

◆ **Writing and giving a speech and thanking all attendants**
The Groom should put thought and effort into his speech before the wedding day. The Groom's speech follows the Father of the Bride's speech and may include the following:

❖ *A thank you to both sets of parents for their support*
❖ *A thank you to the attendants for their hard work before and on the day (whilst the Bride presents the gifts)*
❖ *A thank you to the best man*
❖ *A thank you to all the guests for attending*
❖ *Stories of how the Groom met his wife and how he proposed*
❖ *A toast to the bridesmaids.*

THE BEST MAN

The responsibilities of the best man are:

◆ **Organising the stag weekend**
The Best Man is traditionally responsible for organising the stag party. However, (and perhaps because we have all heard of stag party nightmares), the Groom may not want to hand over the responsibility for this and may decide to organise it himself. There is a separate section in this book to help organise the stag party on page 190.

◆ **Looking after the wedding rings (if there is no ring bearer)**
Probably one of the main reasons the Groom needs to choose a reliable person to be his Best Man is so that he can be responsible for remembering to take the rings with him to the ceremony.

◆ **Making sure the Groom gets to the ceremony**
The Best Man needs to ensure that the Groom gets up early to get ready and is at the ceremony venue in plenty of time for the ceremony.

◆ **Keeping the Groom calm**

As the Groom's 'person to lean on' during the wedding day, the Best Man needs to make sure the Groom stays calm before the ceremony. He can help by sorting out any problems that arise on the morning before the wedding.

◆ **Managing the ushers**

The ushers should be briefed beforehand about their duties on the day of the wedding, however, it is then the Best Man's responsibility to ensure they are conducting these duties as required.

◆ **Best Man's speech**

The Best Man's speech follows on from the Groom's speech. It may include the following:

❖ *Compliments to the Bride, bridesmaids and wedding party*
❖ *How the Best Man knows the Groom*
❖ *How and when the Bride and Groom met*
❖ *How the Groom has changed since meeting the Bride*
❖ *A toast to the Bride and Groom.*

The Best Man has the opportunity to tell funny stories about the Groom. Props such as photographs may also be an amusing addition. However, care should be taken not to offend or upset the audience, in particular the Bride.

The speech should therefore not include the following:

❖ *Previous girlfriends of the Groom or boyfriends of the Bride*
❖ *Negative comments about the day*
❖ *Negative comments about family members of the Bride or Groom.*

◆ **Looking after cards and envelopes on the day**
The Bride and Groom may arrange for a table for guests to put their gifts on. However, the Best Man is usually responsible for collecting cards and envelopes from guests and keeping them safe for the Bride and Groom.

◆ **Looking after the Bride and Groom at the venue and dealing with any problems that arise**
The Best Man (along with the other attendants) is responsible for looking after the Bride and Groom so they are free to enjoy their day. The Best Man should deal with any problems that arise on the day with the help of the Chief Bridesmaid and other family members.

If the Best Man is confident enough, he may also make announcements to ensure guests are seated at the right time and that the Father of the Bride and the Groom are introduced when they give their speeches.

If he is not confident of this task, many reception venues will have members of staff who will be willing to do this or another option might be to hire a Toastmaster.

INSTRUCTIONS FOR THE BEST MAN

Although the Best Man will be briefed before the day, it may be useful to supply him with a list of tasks and useful contact numbers just in case he needs to sort out any problems. This can only be prepared near to the wedding, but if you keep this in mind at the outset you can keep notes of the information you might want to include. Here is an example of a written briefing for the Best Man:

Dear

You have kindly agreed to be Jon's Best Man at our wedding on Saturday 3rd November 20xx. We thought it would be helpful to give you a few pointers on what we need you to do on the day.

1. Jon will need picking up from home at 1.15pm as he has agreed to be in The Royal Oak Pub that is in the centre of Littletown from about 1.30pm to meet the ushers and anyone else who wants to go for a drink before the wedding.

2. If any of the ushers would prefer to go straight to the church, we have asked them to arrive there for about 2.20pm.

---

3. When you arrive at the church, please can you check that the box containing the 'Order of Service' is there and not still in our kitchen at home.

4. Can you also please check with Jackie (the ring bearer) that she has the rings.

5. Alan will be operating the CD player at the church. We have given you spare copies of the CDs in case there is a problem.

6. We are expecting guests to arrive at the reception venue from about 5pm onwards. There will be a drinks reception first before the venue staff will call everyone to be seated. The wedding party will line up just inside the function room.

7. The speeches will take place after the main meal. The Father of the Bride will speak first, followed by Jon and then it will be your turn.

8. Any presents at the reception should be collected up by you at the end of the meal and put in our room.

After that you can relax!

Useful telephone numbers
Jonathan   XXXX XXXX XXXX
Liz   XXXX XXXX XXXX
Reception venue   XXXX XXXX XXXX

Thank you for agreeing to help us with our wedding
ceremony.

We are looking forward to a wonderful day.

Liz & Jonathan

USHERS

The responsibilities of the ushers are as follows:

◆ **Handing out the order of service/ceremony**
The ushers should greet guests as they arrive at the wedding ceremony venue. They should hand out copies of the order of service/ceremony (if there is one) to the guests and give them any other important instructions.

◆ **Instructing which side of the church guests are to sit on**
The Bride's guests traditionally sit on the left and the Groom's guests sit on the right. The ushers should enquire whether the guests belong to the Bride's side or the Groom's side and then show them to their seats.

However, the Bride and Groom may decide they prefer informal seating arrangements.

◆ **Escorting the Bride's mother and Groom's parents to their seats**
As the guests of honour, the Bride's mother and Groom's parents should be escorted to their seats at the front by the ushers.

◆ **Assisting guests with their queries**
The ushers should be briefed on information about the reception, the programme for the day and directions from the ceremony to the venue so they are able to assist other guests if they have any questions.

INSTRUCTIONS FOR THE USHERS

It may be useful to provide the ushers with written instructions and useful contact numbers, which can only be prepared quite near to the wedding date. Here is an example of a written briefing for the ushers:

Dear

You have kindly agreed to be an usher at our wedding on Saturday 3rd November 20xx.

1. We thought it would helpful to give you a few pointers on what we need you to do on the day.

2. Jon will be in The Royal Oak Pub, which is in the centre of Littletown from about 1.30pm so you would be able to meet him there.

3. If you would prefer to go straight to the church, please could you arrive there for about 2.20pm.

4. When you arrive at the church, please can you check that the box containing the 'Order of Service' is there and not still in our kitchen at home.

5. When guests arrive, please ask them if they are on the Bride's side or on the Groom's side. The Bride's guests should be shown to the pews on the left. The Groom's guests should be shown to the pews on the right.

6. There will be enough 'Order of Service' for each guest to have one.

The following guests should be seated in the first few pews at the front of the church.

Please keep the front pews on the right free for:
Jon, his best man and his ring bearer
Jon's Mum and Dad
Jon's sister, Jill and her family
Jon's sister, Susan and her family

Please keep the front pews on the left free for:
Liz's Mum and Dad
Liz's brother, Andrew
Liz's Grandma and her helpers

Useful telephone numbers
Jonathan   XXXX XXXX XXXX
Liz   XXXX XXXX XXXX
Reception Venue   XXXX XXXX XXXX

Thank you for agreeing to help us with our wedding ceremony.

We are looking forward to a wonderful day.

Liz & Jonathan

FATHER OF THE BRIDE

The responsibilities of the Father of the Bride (FOTB) are:

◆ **Paying for reception**
It is traditional for the FOTB to pay for the wedding reception. However, modern couples may feel that this tradition is out dated and it also depends on the financial circumstances of the Bride and Groom and their respective families.

It is important to set out at the beginning who agrees to pay for which parts of the wedding and the maximum amount they are prepared to contribute so there are no misunderstandings and upsets further down the line.

◆ **Payment for other items**
The FOTB may also pay for the wedding dress, bridesmaid's dresses, reception flowers, wedding stationery, the wedding cake, the photographer, transport of the wedding party to the church (except the groom). This should all be discussed beforehand to see if the FOTB or the Bride and Groom will bear the cost.

◆ **Travelling with the Bride to the ceremony**
The FOTB usually travels with the Bride to the ceremony.

◆ **Walking the Bride down the aisle and giving her away to the Groom**
The FOTB usually walks the Bride down the aisle and then gives her away to Groom.

◆ **Taking part in the line up at the reception**
The FOTB is also expected to take part in the line up to greet all the guests as they file into the reception.

◆ **Giving the first speech**
The FOTB is responsible for giving the first speech at the wedding reception. The speech may include the following:

❖ *A welcome to the guests – especially any guests of honour or those who have travelled long distances*
❖ *What the Bride was like when she was a child*
❖ *How meeting the Groom has changed her*
❖ *A welcome to the Groom into the family*
❖ *Advice on a long and happy marriage*
❖ *A toast to the Bride and Groom*

FATHER OF THE GROOM

The responsibilities of the Father of the Groom (FOTG) are:

◆ **Taking part in the line up at the reception**
As part of the wedding party up the FOTG is also expected to take part in the line up to greet all the guests as they file into the reception.

Although the FOTG has fewer responsibilities than the FOTB, he may decide to contribute financially to the reception, for example, offering to pay for the drinks.

CHAPTER 2

YOUR GUESTS

Before you start the search for your venue for your wedding ceremony and your reception, it is a good idea to create an initial guest list so that you have an idea of the numbers of guests you are expecting in order to find a venue that can accommodate them all.

5 steps to Creating your Guest List

1. Start by listing all the members of your family and friends you would like to invite.

2. Ask both sets of parents to do the same.

3. Create a master list of all the potential guests under the following headings. Remember to include partners and children.

	Bride	Groom
Bride & Groom		
Family		
Parents		
Siblings		
Grandparents		
Aunts/Uncles		
Cousins		

	Bride	**Groom**
Wedding Party		
Best man		
Chief Bridesmaid		
Ushers		
Bridesmaids		
Friends		
Close friends		

	Bride	Groom
Childhood friends		
College friends		
Work friends		
Guests of the Bride and Groom's parents		

4. Once you have looked at suitable venues, check to see if the number of people on the list can be accommodated at your ideal venue.

You may find that if your network of friends and family is very extensive you will need to reduce the number of guests on your list. Here are a few ideas for helping you to decide who to include:

❖ *Think about who will sit next to whom at the wedding reception. Remember that the Bride and Groom tend to be very busy on their wedding day chatting to all their guests, so if there are people who aren't going to know anyone else, will they be outgoing enough to chat to new people or would they feel uncomfortable not knowing anyone?*

❖ *Think about not inviting children to the wedding. Although this may seem like a tough decision and children would give the event a very different feel, you may be surprised to find that some of your guests would prefer to find a baby sitter for their children so they can let their hair down at the wedding reception.*

❖ *Are there people in your list that both the Bride and Groom can decide not to invite? For example, if you both choose not to invite anyone from your place of work, you can let your work colleagues know that your wedding is going to be for family and close friends only, and due to a limited capacity at the venue you have had to make difficult decisions about your guest list. Most people should understand, especially those who have been involved in wedding preparations before. As an alternative, you could organise a night out or a meal out with your work colleagues before the wedding so that you still celebrate the occasion with them.*

5. Create your final guest list – see page 45. If you have a capacity limit at your venue, make sure the list does not exceed this. If your guest list contains exactly the same number of guests as your venue capacity limit, have a reserve list too. It is likely that not all your guests will be able to come to your wedding due to other commitments, holidays, difficulties travelling etc. Therefore, you may be able to invite some of the guests that you did not manage to fit on the original list. However, you will need to take **extreme care** if you are going to invite people on the reserve list to make sure they do not feel upset that they were not on the original list.

GUEST LIST

If you have computer skills, creating a spreadsheet can help make life a lot easier to monitor your guest list.

If you group the guests in your list according to the following categories and shade each group in a different colour it makes it easier to see how many guests there are in each group.

- ❖ Wedding party
- ❖ Bride's family and friends of Bride's parents
- ❖ Groom's family and friends of Groom's parents
- ❖ Bride and Groom's friends

This could come in useful if you need to reduce guest numbers to fit them into the venue or to meet your budget.

Name	No of guests invited	Address 1	Address 2	Address 3	Postcode	Replied to invitation	No of guests attending	Names of guests attending (for seating plan)	Dietary requirements
Miss Elizabeth Myers (the Bride)	1						1	Mrs Elizabeth Frost	
Mr Jonathan Frost (the Groom)	1						1	Mr Jonathan Frost	
Mr & Mrs M Myers	2						2	Mr Michael Myers Mrs Kazia Myers	
Mr & Mrs P Frost	2						2	Mr Peter Frost Mrs Jean Frost	
Mr Andrew Myers	1						1	Mr Andrew Myers	
Mr & Mrs B Roberts	2						2	Mr Brett Roberts Mrs Marilyn Roberts	
Mr & Mrs Kirby & Sarah	3						3	Mr David Kirby Mrs Liz Kirby Miss Sarah Kirby	
Mr & Mrs T Morley, George & Max	4						4	Mr Tim Morley Mrs Jill Morley Master George Morley Master Max Morley	
Mr & Mrs C Knifton, Daniel & Hilary	4						4	Mr Charles Knifton Mrs Susan Knifton Master Daniel Knifton Miss Hilary Knifton	
Mr & Mrs A Green	2						2	Mr Alan Green Mrs Deborah Green	
Dr Zoe Read & Mr Lee Davis	2						2	Dr Zoe Read Mr Lee Davis	
Total									

CHAPTER 3

THE CEREMONY

One of the first decisions you will need to make about your wedding is where to have the actual wedding ceremony.

In England (and Wales), you can get married at the following places if you are a UK citizen:

◆ Register Office
◆ A venue approved for civil marriages
◆ Church of England
◆ Some other religious buildings (provided that the person marrying the couple is allowed by law to do so).

If you choose to get married at a Register Office you should contact the staff there who will advise you on the procedure of booking the correct date and time for your wedding. They will also advise you on all the formalities associated with giving notice of your intention to marry, the documents you will need to produce, the fees you will need to pay and the necessary timescale to allow.

If you choose to get married at a venue approved for civil marriages, you should contact the venue to make a reservation and staff there will advise you on which Register Office to contact regarding the legal formalities.

If you are having a Church of England (or Church in Wales) wedding ceremony, you will need to contact the parish minister/vicar of the church you want to get married in. They will advise you on steps you need to take to ensure you can get married on the day you have chosen and comply with marriage legalities.

For a marriage ceremony in a religious building (e.g. a church other than the Church of England, a mosque or a temple), you should contact the religious leader for advice on the correct procedures you should follow. It may be necessary to have a register office ceremony to be legally married but this can be followed by a religious ceremony later.

Scotland has its owns laws regarding marriage so if you are proposing to get married in Scotland, contact the venue for advice on what steps you need to take.

The marriage laws are different in different countries, therefore in every case, the best advice is to contact the church/venue/religious building where you would like to get married. You should ask for advice on what you need to do, the documents you will need to provide, the fees you need to pay and whether it is possible for you to get married there. Staff at the places licensed for wedding ceremonies will be used to advising couples.

◆ **Questions to ask the Church Minister or Registrar**

Will you be available to marry us on the date,
   time and location we want to get married?   Yes ☐   No ☐

Will you be able to/be willing to marry us?   Yes ☐   No ☐

What is the fee?   £_____

What is the procedure we need to follow
   to be able to marry?

Will it be possible to have a rehearsal?   Yes ☐   No ☐

   If so, on what date and at which time?   Date:
                                              Time:

Is there a sample wedding ceremony
   we can use?   Yes ☐   No ☐

Are there any restrictions on the readings
   we can have?   Yes ☐   No ☐

If so, what are the restrictions?

Will we be able to have music at the ceremony?   Yes ☐   No ☐

Are there any restrictions on the type of music?

If so, what are the restrictions?   Yes ☐   No ☐

You will probably need to start looking for a reception venue at the same time as you start to arrange your wedding ceremony. Until you have confirmation that your wedding ceremony can take place on the date and at the time you propose, keep the reception venue booking as provisional but keep in touch with the reception venue to let them know how you are getting on with arrangements and when you will be able to confirm the booking.

CHAPTER 4

THE RECEPTION VENUE

5 STEPS TO SELECTING A RECEPTION VENUE

1. Location

If you have decided on the location for your wedding ceremony, discuss how close you need the reception venue to be. You need to consider the following:

* *How well do the guests know the area*
* *Will the guests be able to transport themselves easily between the ceremony and reception venue*
* *The time it will take for you and your guests to travel.*

Decide on a maximum travel time and distance and keep your search within those boundaries.

2. Initial Search

Once you have decided on the area, use as many methods as possible to search for a venue, such as:

* *Internet*
* *Directories – e.g. local telephone directories*
* *Local Press – some venues advertise function rooms*
* *Local wedding publications*
* *Wedding fairs*
* *Word of Mouth – ask family members, friends, work colleagues. Most people will have attended a function in the last few months and may be able to recommend some options.*

3. Gather Information

Depending on the area and how many venues there are in total, choose a number of venues that you initially like the look of (around 6 – 8) and contact them for more information on their prices for room hire, catering, drinks etc.

Many venues will have a pack they can send you in the post. Some will ask for the date of your wedding to check availability at the outset as venues get booked up very far in advance.

4. Make a Shortlist

Based on the information you have gathered so far reduce your list to 3 – 5 venues that seem to meet some or most of your criteria, for example, capacity, price, location.

Book an appointment to view these venues to see how you feel about them when you visit them.

The following grid should help you to compare the venues:

Venue Comparison Grid	Ideal Venue	Venue A
Number of guests accommodated Day / Evening		
Type of venue (Modern/traditional/quirky)		
Layout of venue (one room or function room and separate bar)		
Distance from ceremony		
Availability		
Venue hire fee 　Price per head for 　3 Course Meal 　Fork Buffet 　Barbecue 　Evening Finger Buffet 　Drinks Package		
Corkage fee (if venue allows Bride and Groom to supply wine/champagne)		
Any other charges		
Overnight accommodation on site		
Price		
Child friendly venue		
Parking for guests		
Personal feeling about venue (can you imagine you and your guests there)		

Venue B	Venue C	Venue D	Venue E

5. Select your Venue

Once you have compared the venues available, you can then make a selection and provisionally book the venue. Only confirm the booking once the details of your wedding ceremony are also confirmed. However, it is useful to keep in touch with the venue to let them know of progress.

ADDITIONAL TIPS ABOUT BOOKING THE RECEPTION VENUE

Always check with the venue manager about public liability insurance, certificates of food hygiene (for in-house catering) and licensing issues regarding the sale of alcohol and entertainment. Ask to see the certificates if you are unsure of anything.

When you confirm the booking make sure you have all the arrangements in writing and understand the terms and conditions.

The written confirmation or contract should include:

❖ *The date of the wedding reception.*
❖ *Cost of venue hire.*
❖ *How long you have the function room for.*
❖ *Cost of food per head.*
❖ *Menu choices.*
❖ *Cost of drinks per head.*
❖ *Drinks choices.*
❖ *The minimum number of guests you will have to pay for.*
❖ *The date by which you must pay any deposit.*
❖ *The dates by which you must pay any further instalments.*
❖ *The date by which you must pay the balance of money due to the venue.*

❖ *The date by which you need to advise final guest numbers (and special dietary requirements).*

❖ *What you will have to pay if you cancel the reception.*

❖ *What the venue will do if they cancel the reception (for reasons beyond their control).*

It may also include details such as:

❖ *Guest rate for overnight accommodation*

❖ *Any additional charges.*

The written contract should contain the basic information regarding payment and guest numbers, but as you will find out nearer the time of your wedding there will be a lot of additional details that you will need to agree with staff at the hotel, e.g. arrangements for the cake, delivery of flowers etc. Although venues that regularly hold wedding receptions will have staff to help you with these arrangements, if you create your own planner document, you can be prepared for any meetings you might have and give a lot of thought beforehand to how you want things to run.

The document on page 72 can be adapted to suit your function but will give you a good starting point. There is an example document followed by a blank document for your own use.

You can also give copies of the completed documents to a couple of reliable family members or friends so that they can oversee things are going smoothly on the day.

Some Information about Marquees

If finding your ideal venue is proving a difficult task, you may want to consider hiring a marquee.

This can be a suitable option if you are finding it difficult to find a venue of a suitable size for your guests. Some reception venues or restaurants may offer a marquee as an alternative option if their function room is small.

However, it is worth considering whether a marquee is going to be suitable for the time of year you are getting married. It is possible for weather to be unpredictable at any time, which could cause problems if gales or flash floods hit on your wedding day.

Although a marquee may provide a solution regarding how to accommodate your guests there are many things you will need to consider.

1. **Where are you going to have your marquee?**
   Will it be in the grounds of a venue? Do you know of anyone with a field they can rent to you? Do you have any friends or family members with a large back garden? In each case you are going to need to ask permission from the owner of the land to erect a marquee and ensure you comply with any legal requirements if you do this.

If the marquee is going to be erected specifically for your wedding (rather than using one that is permanently available for hire at a venue) you will need to check when it can be put up and taken down and check the owner of the land is happy with the timetable. You may need it to be constructed a few days before the event to give you time to decorate it.

You will also need to think about clearing up after the event. Who will be responsible for leaving the site at you found it? As the Bride and Groom are likely to be leaving on their honeymoon shortly after the reception, this needs to be delegated to someone trustworthy.

2. **How are you going to cater for your guests?**
   If the marquee is in the grounds of a venue or even attached to the venue by an entrance hall/tunnel, it may be possible for the venue caterers to cook and serve the food to your guests. However, if you are considering having a marquee elsewhere you will need to consult with your caterers as to how they will be able to cook for your guests and what equipment they will require to enable them to create an 'off-site' kitchen. It may be useful to discuss this with the marquee company to see if there are any caterers they could recommend who are used to this sort of catering.

3. **How are you going to get a power supply to the marquee?**
   You will need to discuss power supply requirements with the company you are hiring the marquee from to ensure you have

enough power for lighting and other requirements e.g. catering and disco/band. You will need to check what their policy is regarding a back up in case the power fails.

4. **How are you going to organise things to make your guests comfortable?**
When discussing requirements for the marquee, you will need to consider furniture requirements including seating and tables. Depending on the time of year, you may need heating in the marquee too.

You will also need to consider arrangements you will make regarding toilets. If your marquee is near or connected to a venue such as a hotel, your guests may be able to use their facilities but if it is, for example, in a field you will need to consider hiring portable toilets.

Another area to consider is whether your guests will have to spend time outside the marquee, for example, if they need to walk to use toilet facilities etc. If this is the case, you will need to consider supplying umbrellas in case of rain.

Will there be cloakroom facilities for your guests to hang coats etc?

Where will people stay overnight? Can they easily get to the overnight accommodation from the site?

5. **Are you going to have a drinks bar?**
   Again, if the marquee is in the grounds of a venue, the staff may be able to organise a drinks bar in the marquee. Alternatively, there are companies that will supply mobile bars. However, you will need to ensure you comply with relevant legislation regarding provision and sale of alcohol.

6. **Does everything comply with legislation?**
   There are many areas of legislation that your suppliers need to comply with. These include health and safety, fire risks, food handling and hygiene, supply of alcohol and noise. You will need to check with all your suppliers to ensure everything you are planning to do is compliant with current laws. (This is good general advice as well as advice specific to hiring a marquee.)

7. **Who is going to ensure the reception runs smoothly?**
   If the marquee is associated with a venue, the staff at the venue should be able to ensure all is running to schedule. However, if this is not the case, it may be worth speaking to the caterers to see if they are able to manage proceedings or hire the services of an events planner.

SEATING PLANS

Top Table

The traditional top table plan is shown below. However, due to changing times and family structures, it is important for the Bride and Groom to consider who to sit on the top table. Below is a blank template for you to fill in.

Chief Bridesmaid	Groom's Father	Bride's Mother	Groom	Bride	Bride's Father	Groom's Mother	Best Man
◯	◯	◯	◯	◯	◯	◯	◯

TABLE PLANS

Table plans and room layout all depend on your venue, the size and shape of tables and the number of guests you are having.

Here are some examples of table layouts which may be adapted to your own reception.

Your venue will be able to advise you on options.

If you have a small number of guests it may be possible to arrange the tables so everyone is facing each other:

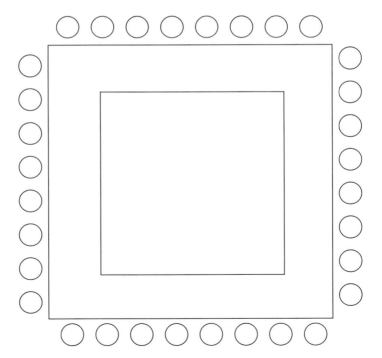

Another alternative is to have rectangular tables sideways on to the top table:

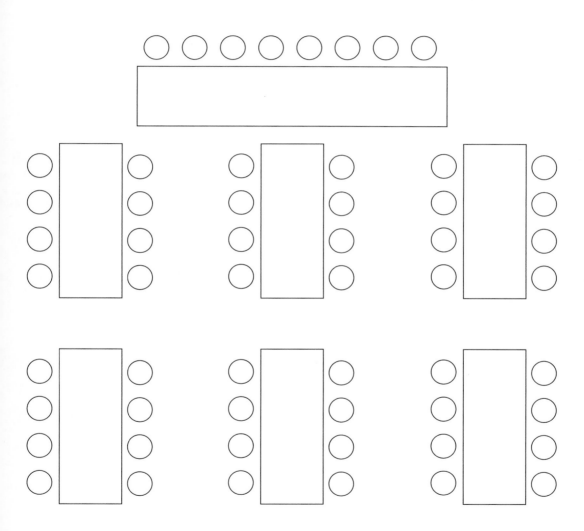

Another alternative for rectangular tables is to position them at an angle towards the top table:

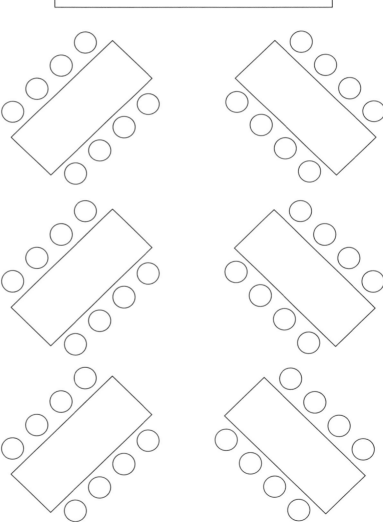

If the venue has round tables, these tend to be scattered in front
of the top table:

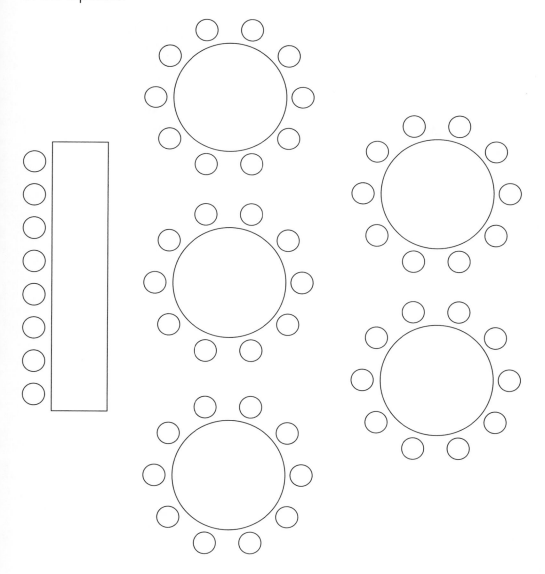

TABLE NUMBERS

Table numbers are being used less frequently as the Bride and Groom often do not want to make guests feel less important if they are sat at the tables with the highest numbers.

One way round this is to alter the table arrangement so that the table numbers are not in order. See example below:

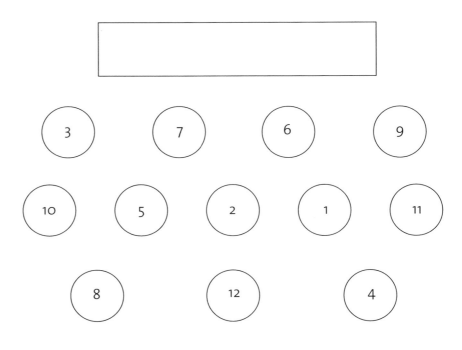

Another popular way is to name the tables. Couples might decide to choose names that fit with the theme of their wedding. (See chapter 7 on the wedding theme.)

For example, an Italian themed wedding may have tables named after Italian cities such as Rome, Venice, Florence etc.

Couples may choose a favourite film title for each table.

Make sure you find out from the venue what the maximum number of people that can sit at the top table and at the other tables so you can consider this when arranging your guests on the seating plan.

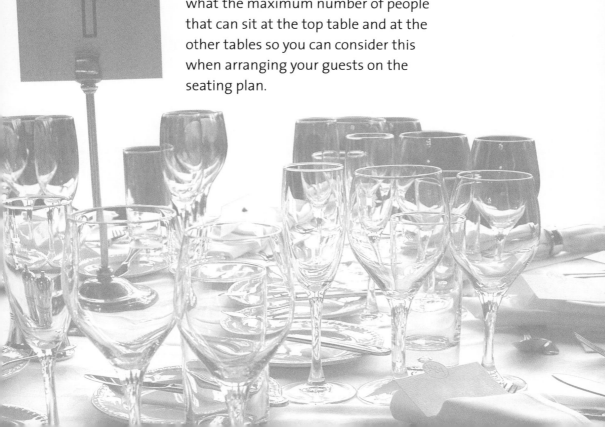

Master Planner for Venue

Date of Wedding: 3rd November 20XX

Bride: Liz Myers   Tel:.................................   Email: ....
Groom: Jon Frost   Tel:.................................   Email: ....

Item	Details	Contact
Programme for the day	15.00 Wedding ceremony at Littletown Church 16.00 Photographs with guests 16.30 Guests leave for venue 17.00 Guests arrive at venue for drinks reception, line up and then 17.30 Guests sit for 3 course meal 19.30 Speeches 20.00 Evening guests arrive and disco starts 21.00 Bacon sandwiches and wedding cake 00.30 Bar closes	
Day Catering	3 course meal Starter: Farmhouse Paté on toast Main: Farmhouse grill, new potatoes, salad Dessert: Apple pie with cream or custard Served to 138 guests Vegetarian option: Char-grilled vegetable terrine, brie and broccoli pastry parcel Served to 5 guests	

Item	Details	Contact
	2 babies – high chairs needed – parents to bring own food.	
	143 guests @ £X per head	
	5 children's meals 5 @ £X per head	
Day Drinks	Drinks reception when guests arrive Buck's Fizz or Orange Juice (Buck's Fizz for two-thirds of guests/ Orange Juice for one-third)	
	143 guests @ £X per head	
	Champagne toast during speeches	
	143 guests @ £X per head	
Evening Catering	Bacon sandwiches for 150 guests	
	150 guests @ £X per head	
Cake	Cake to be delivered at 4pm on 02/11/20XX By Liz	
	Stand to be delivered with the cake	

Item	Details	Contact
	Staff at venue are to assemble cake Cake knife to be provided by the venue Cake to be displayed on separate table covered in ivory linen cloth to the right of the top table during day reception. Cake to be taken away and cut at 21.30 and wrapped in burgundy serviettes. Cake to be placed on trays on tables for guests to take.	
Decorations	Tables to be covered in ivory linen cloths 3 balloon clusters – ivory and burgundy – to be delivered – one cluster per table (15 in total) Delivery at 11am on 03/11/20XX By the Balloon Making Company Decorations for tables to be delivered by Bride on 02/11/20XX which will be Wedding favours Name cards Menu cards Disposable cameras Confetti	XXXX XXXXXX

Item	Details	Contact
Flowers	Flowers will be delivered by The Flower Arranging Company on 02/11/20XX at midday The arrangements will be One oval shaped arrangement for the top table 14 table centre arrangements Cake top for wedding cake 2 bouquets for gifts – to be kept hidden until the speeches	XXXX XXXXXX
DJ	DJ to arrive at 18.30 to set up. Booked through the DJ Company Bride and Groom's first dance at 20.30 Song – to be decided	XXXX XXXXXX

Master Planner for Venue

Date of Wedding:

Bride: .... Tel: .... Email: ....
Groom: .... Tel: .... Email: ....

Item	Details	Contact
Programme for the day		
Day Catering		

Item	Details	Contact
Day Drinks		
Evening Catering		
Cake		

Item	Details	Contact
Decorations		
Flowers		
DJ		

Item	Details	Contact
Other arrangements		

CHAPTER 5

CATERING

When looking for your venue, you will also need to consider what type of food you would like to serve for your guests and at what times.

If you keep in mind the theme for your wedding, you can select food that will complement the atmosphere you are trying to create.

Some venues will offer in-house catering for your reception. If a venue is able to supply catering in-house, they are unlikely to allow other caterers into their kitchens. In certain circumstances they may allow external caterers, e.g. if food must be prepared in a certain way for religious reasons. However, the venue may charge a fee for using their kitchen facilities.

If your venue does not provide in-house catering, you will need to engage the services of an external caterer. It may be a good idea to ask at the venue whether there are any businesses that have provided catering at the venue before. If a caterer regularly supplies a venue, they are more likely to be familiar with the facilities and have greater knowledge of what is available on site so that they can ensure they bring any necessary equipment with them.

They may also be used to providing table linen suitable for the furniture at the venue.

KEY DECISIONS TO MAKE

Will you want to serve light snacks to your
guests whilst the photographs are taken?   Yes ☐   No ☐

If yes, what would you like to serve?

What type of food are you hoping to serve at your day time reception?	3 course – table service	☐
	Hot fork buffet	☐
	Cold fork buffet	☐
	Finger buffet	☐
	Barbecue	☐
	Other	☐
What type of food are you hoping to serve at your evening reception?	3 course – table service	☐
	Hot fork buffet	☐
	Cold fork buffet	☐
	Finger buffet	☐
	Barbecue	☐
	Other	☐

QUESTIONS TO ASK THE CATERING MANAGER

What type of food can you provide?

And at what price per head?

3 course – table service	£_____
Hot fork buffet	£_____
Cold fork buffet	£_____
Finger buffet	£_____
Barbecue	£_____
Other	£_____

Can you give us some menus to show what type of food you can supply?

Are the following items included in the price?

Table linen	Yes ☐	No ☐
Crockery	Yes ☐	No ☐
Cutlery	Yes ☐	No ☐
Glassware	Yes ☐	No ☐
Waitressing staff	Yes ☐	No ☐
Staff to clear up	Yes ☐	No ☐
Other	_____	

Can you supply vegetarian options?   Yes ☐   No ☐

Can you supply separate meals for people with specific dietary requirements?	Yes ☐	No ☐
Is it cheaper to choose a set menu for our guests?	Yes ☐	No ☐
If we set a budget per head, can you provide a menu option for that price?	Yes ☐	No ☐
Is it possible to come and see a function you are providing the catering for?	Yes ☐	No ☐
Can we taste the food before the event?	Yes ☐	No ☐

If the caterers are not based at the venue, you may want to consider asking the following questions in addition to the questions above.

What time will you arrive at the venue?		
Do you clean up after the function?	Yes ☐	No ☐
Have you catered at this venue before?	Yes ☐	No ☐
Will you be willing to visit the venue with us beforehand to check the facilities are suitable for the type of catering we require?		
What is your contingency plan if something goes wrong beyond your control? (e.g. van breakdown)		

If a venue allows you to bring your own drinks but is unable to supply glassware it may be possible for the caterers to supply this and also assist with pouring and serving of drinks for your guests. You will need to check if there is a cost attached to this. Always ensure you can comply with relevant legislation regarding provision and sale of alcohol.

Always check with the caterers about public liability insurance and certificates of food hygiene. Ask to see certificates.

ADDITIONAL TIPS FOR BOOKING THE CATERING

If you are booking the catering through an external catering company rather than through the venue itself, when you confirm the booking make sure you have all the arrangements in writing and understand the terms and conditions.

The written confirmation or contract should include:-

❖ *The date of the wedding reception*
❖ *The venue name and address*
❖ *Menu choices*
❖ *Cost of food per head*
❖ *The minimum number of guests you will have to pay for*
❖ *The date by which you must pay any deposit*
❖ *The dates by which you must pay any further instalments*
❖ *The date by which you must pay the balance of money due to the venue*
❖ *The date by which you need to advise final guest numbers (and special dietary requirements)*
❖ *What you will have to pay if you cancel the reception*
❖ *What the caterers will do if they cancel the catering (for reasons beyond their control).*

Keeping within Budget

There will not be many times in your life when you are responsible for feeding (and paying for) so many guests on one day. As food is usually charged per head, your final bill will be directly proportional to the number of people you invite.

However, if you cannot cut your guest list, you can still get the most value for money from your catering budget by carefully considering what you actually give your guests to eat and the times at which you feed them.

Here are a few ideas that other people have used in the past:

◆ If you are going to have a sit-down reception during the day, it is possible to reduce the cost by choosing a cold fork buffet rather than a hot sit down meal. Cold food tends to be easier and cheaper to produce. It can be prepared off-site and transported in refrigerated vans by caterers and therefore can still be supplied even if kitchen facilities are limited. Having a buffet also reduces the amount of serving staff needed. However, the food can be prepared to look fantastic and colourful with centre pieces such as dressed salmon or carved cold meats.

◆ If you decide on a sit-down three course meal for your reception, consider altering the menu to a starter, main course and serve your wedding cake for dessert. If the starter and the main course are substantial, your guests will not miss a separate dessert and those with a sweet tooth will still have cake, and it could save you money.

◆ Both the barbecue and finger buffet options tend to be cheaper than formal sit-down meals or fork buffets. If you time your reception for early evening and choose these catering options, it could work out more economical than having a formal sit-down reception during the day followed by an evening reception.

◆ If you choose a venue such as a restaurant or hotel, ask for the various menu options available and check if choosing a set menu or food that is in season can work out more cost effective.

◆ Ask what menu options can be created for a set price per head.

◆ If you are looking for something a little different to a traditional English reception, perhaps you might want to consider Asian food or other international cuisines as an alternative (although this will depend upon your location in the UK as to how feasible this is).

◆ If you are happy to try something more quirky, think about offering your guests fish and chips or sausage and mash. It could be a good talking point for your wedding. Another option is to give your guests bacon sandwiches as an alternative to a finger buffet in the evening.

WEDDING CAKE

The choice of wedding cake is something personal to the Bride and Groom but in recent times, choices have become more varied. Couples can now opt for sponge or chocolate cake instead of the traditional fruitcake. Some couples are beginning to alter traditions by not having a cake at all but replacing the cake with a chocolate fountain or an alternative centrepiece.

Wedding cake designs are becoming more lavish and intricate. The more elaborate the design, the higher the price.

In order to decide on the type of cake you would like to have, there are a few basic questions to answer at the outset:

What type of cake would you prefer?		
	Fruit cake	☐
	Sponge cake	☐
	Chocolate cake	☐
	Mixed layers to give a choice	☐
	Other _____	

How many tiers would you like?		
	One tier	☐
	Two tier	☐
	Three tier	☐
	Other _____	

What other decoration are
you looking for?

Bride & Groom	☐
Decorative piping	☐
Sugar flowers	☐
Artificial flowers	☐
Real flowers	☐
Other	_____

OPTIONS FOR THE CAKE

◆ **Wedding Cake Designer**

This is probably the most obvious choice of where to find your
wedding cake and if you consult your local telephone directory or
search the internet, it is likely you will find a number of
professional wedding cake designers/makers. Some internet sites
show photographs of different design options that can be very
helpful when trying to make up your mind on the type of cake you
are looking for.

If you choose this option, you will need to talk to the cake maker
about how you want the cake designed and how it will fit into the
theme of your wedding. They will also need to know how many
people you will want to give portions of the cake to. This would
include your guests and anyone else you would like to distribute
cake to after the wedding day.

It may be difficult to understand why a cake made up of flour, eggs, sugar and raisins can end up costing several hundreds of pounds. However, there is considerable skill involved in icing a cake as well as the number of hours involved in creating one of the showpieces and focal points of your wedding day. If the cake maker is producing extra decorations for the cake such as sugar roses, this is very time consuming and requires a lot of detailed work.

If you find that having the cake of your choice turns out to be costly, speak to your cake maker about having a smaller version for display. You may be able to supplement your wedding cake with additional cutting cake (iced wedding cake produced in rectangular blocks which can be sliced up and served to your guests, but which is not actually part the 'the wedding cake'.) If the cake maker is unable to supply this, you may be able to buy cutting cake from a local supermarket.

Ask the cake maker if you can taste some cake too.

◆ **Bakery**

Your local high street bakery may be able to supply wedding cakes. Many have sample cakes in their shop windows. It will depend on each individual bakery as to how ornate they would be able to make the cake.

◆ **Supermarkets**

Many supermarkets now supply basic iced fruit and sponge cakes in various sizes. It is also possible to buy pillars so the layers can be assembled into a tiered cake. The packaging often gives ideas on suitable decorations to add to the top of the cake. However, if you are using a florist for your flowers, it may be possible to ask them to produce a floral cake top to keep the theme the same. (The florist will need to ensure any flowers/foliage coming into contact with the cake have not been treated with any harmful chemicals/pesticides that could be transferred to the cake).

Prices vary between supermarkets so it is worth shopping around. In my experience, it is not always the most expensive cakes that taste the best. This option also gives you the advantage of buying the smallest sized cake layer so you can taste the cake beforehand.

In addition to the official display cake, most supermarkets will also sell rectangular iced cutting cakes. These can be sponge or fruitcake. This gives you the option of opting for a smaller wedding cake but still being able to supply enough cake for all your guests, as well as offering them a choice of fruit or sponge cake.

As an alternative to the above, there are some internet-based companies through which you can order basic iced cakes as well as decorations. If you decide on this route, it is advisable to order sample products in advance to make sure you receive what you are expecting.

◆ **Friends/relatives**

Do you have a relative who would be able to make a cake for you? This could cut the cost considerably or may even be offered as a wedding present. But you need to be absolutely sure they are confident to do the job and will not let you down.

◆ **Other options**

If you are looking for something less traditional, another option is to create a cake made up of tiers of cupcakes on a suitable cake stand. Some companies specialise in hand crafted cupcakes with sugar flowers on top. Although these are stunning they can be very costly. However, supermarkets can stock iced cupcakes at various times of the year with a variety of designs such as flowers on them made out of sugar paste. It is worth having a look to see what is being supplied.

A variation of this theme which would be suitable for a winter wedding is a tiered display of mince pies. If these are dusted with icing sugar and decorated with sprigs of holly and other seasonal foliage, this could make a very attractive alternative to a traditional cake.

Profiteroles piled up into a tower could also be an alternative option.

You will need to work out how many pieces of cake you need for your guests and also to send out to people who are unable to attend the wedding.

If you are dealing with a cake maker or bakery they should be able to give you an idea of the number of portions you will be able to get from the cake you are ordering when they discuss your requirements with you.

If you are buying a cake from a supermarket, there should be guidelines on numbers of portions with the cake.

If you are asking someone to make the cake for you, you will need to consult with them on the size to ensure you can get enough portions for all your guests.

The actual number of portions will obviously depend on the size of the slices and how the cake is cut: You also need to remember that if you have a sponge cake and a fruit cake of the same size, you will get approximately two slices of sponge cake for every 3 slices of fruit cake. For example, if a fruit cake produced 15 slices, you would get about 10 slices from a sponge cake of the same size.

Whichever option you choose, you will also need to enquire/think about the following:

How the cake will be presented?
     Will the cake maker supply a stand?
     Will you need to hire one?
     Will you need to buy pillars to have
        the cake tiers assembled on top
        of one another?	

When will the cake be ready for collection?
     Will you pick it up?
     Will someone else pick it up for you?	

Are there any special considerations when transporting the cake?	
Will the reception venue provide a cake knife or should you arrange for this?	
When will the cake be taken to the venue?	

How and where will the cake be stored
     at the venue?
     (This will need to be suitable for the
     type of cake, for example, a chocolate
     cake on a hot day could melt)	

Who will assemble the cake at the venue?	
Where and how will you want the cake displayed?	

In addition, when speaking to the venue manager or the catering manager, you will need to give clear instructions to the person responsible for assembling the cake.

If the wedding is taking place in summer, it will be necessary to keep the cake in a cool place for as long as possible so there is less risk of the cake collapsing in the heat. In particular, if the cake is decorated in chocolate or with chocolate flowers, it would be a pity if these melted before guests had a chance to see the cake.

CHAPTER 6

WHAT TO WEAR

FOR THE BRIDE

The wedding dress is probably the first thing every Bride thinks about when they start planning the wedding. As it is the Bride's role to be the centre of attention for the whole day, a lot of emphasis is put upon what the Bride should wear.

A well known superstition is that it is bad luck for the Groom to see the Bride's dress before the wedding day. Therefore, it is one area where the Groom is usually not consulted.

The checklist in this chapter is designed to give you a starting point in deciding what style and type of outfit you would like.

What type of dress would you like?	Traditional	☐
	Modern	☐
Would you prefer	Two piece (bodice and skirt)	☐
	Dress	☐
What neckline would you like?	Strapless	☐
	Sweet heart	☐
	Scoop round	☐
	Halter neck	☐
	V neckline	☐
	Off shoulder – V neckline	☐
	Other _____	

What type of sleeves would you like?	Sleeveless	☐
	Straps	☐
	Cap/short sleeves	☐
	Long sleeves	☐
	Other _____	
What type of skirt would you like?	Straight	☐
	A line	☐
	Fishtail	☐
	Ball gown/ Full skirt	☐
	Skirt length: _____	
What sort of train would you like?	None	☐
	Short	☐
	Medium	☐
	Long	☐
What colour dress would you like?	White	☐
	Ivory	☐
	Cream	☐
	Other _____	
Is there additional detail you would like?	Beading	☐
	Embroidery	☐
	Sequins	☐
	Lace	☐
	Other _____	

Is there a particular fabric you would like your dress to be made of?	Silk	☐
	Satin	☐
	Organza	☐
	Chiffon	☐
	Tulle	☐
	Other _____	

What other accessories are you planning to wear with the dress? (NB it is important to consult your hairdresser about hairstyles available for you with the accessories you wish to wear.)	Tiara	☐
	Veil	☐
	Jewellery _____	

Also remember to find suitable
lingerie to wear with your dress

Once you have had an initial look at this checklist, here are a few
other tips on how to find the dress of your dreams.

1. Look through wedding magazines and search the internet to
   get some ideas of what you think you might want to find. Start
   collecting examples of photographs of the dress styles you are
   looking for.

2. Book a day in your diary to visit some bridal shops as an initial
   dress trial. If this is a Saturday make sure you book an
   appointment. Many bridal shops will be very busy so without an
   appointment you may not be able to go in and try dresses on or
   you may not get adequate attention from the shop assistant.

3. Take any pictures or samples of what you think you are looking for with you. However, when you go to the bridal shops try to be open minded and try a range of different styles. You may be surprised to find that the styles you have in mind may be very different to what you feel most comfortable in when you try dresses on.

4. Take your mother and/or your sister and/or your friend. You may decide that on your first visit to the bridal shops you want to go alone to clarify what you want first, without being influenced by anyone else who may have strong ideas about what you should be wearing. But taking a couple of people you are close to and who you trust may help get a balanced view on which dresses suit you best.

5. Trying on wedding dresses can be very exciting and enjoyable and you will get a flavour of what it is like to be the centre of attention. However, beware of the sales assistant's flattering comments. It is their job to try to encourage you to buy the most expensive dress possible, so they may not always have your best interests at heart. Therefore, by taking people you trust with you, you will be able to get a more balanced view of what suits you.

6. Go with your 'gut' feeling. People always say that the Bride knows when she finds the right dress and your instincts will drive you in the right direction.

Paste scraps of materials and photos here.

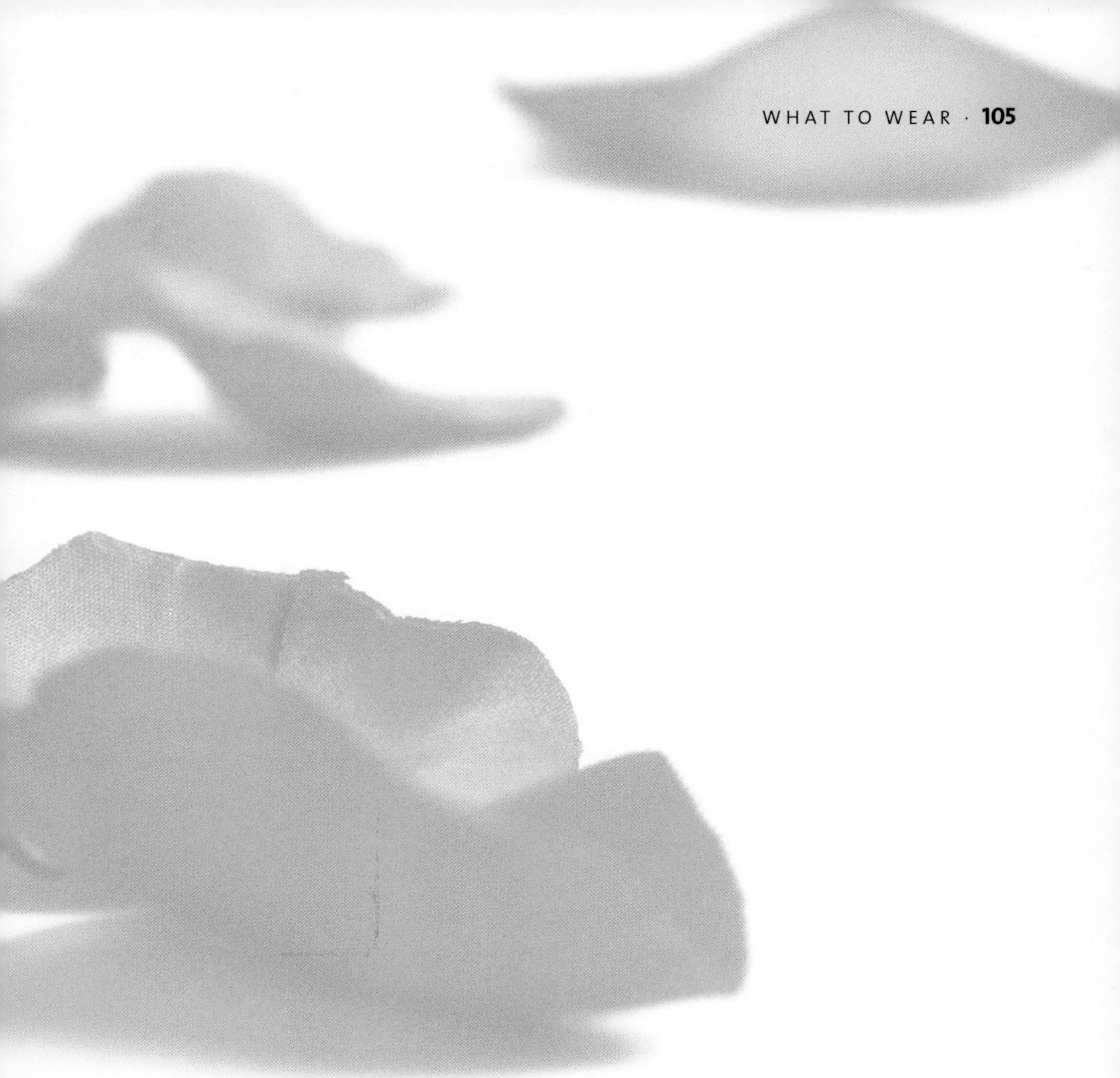

KEEPING WITHIN BUDGET

Your wedding dress is probably going to be one of the most expensive items of clothing you will ever buy – especially when you consider the price it costs per hour of wearing it. If you have a strict budget for your dress, you may want to consider some of these options when looking for your dress:-

◆ If your dress is made to order, some bridal shops will charge an extra 'rushed order' fee if you order the dress less than six months before your wedding day. Therefore, by being organised you can save some money.

◆ If you wait for the sales in wedding dress shops, it may be possible to pick up a bargain. If you start looking for your dress early, you could enquire in your local bridal shops to see when the next sale is likely to be.

◆ Following all the publicity about the high cost of weddings, many high street stores and supermarkets now offer ranges of bridal wear. The options available are often quite simple but elegant and could be personalised by using accessories.

◆ Check the small ads in your local paper for a second-hand dress.

◆ Check auction web-sites to look for a second hand dress. (But take care as the photo provided on the site and the final product may look very different.) Check the item description, read the feedback comments about the seller and ask the seller any questions you have before bidding.

◆ Research the types of fabric that suit the style of dress you like. The type of fabric you choose could have a big impact on the overall price of your dress.

◆ Carefully consider the style of dress you would like. If you choose a style that requires a lot of fabric e.g. a dress with a long train or a full skirt, the price will increase.

◆ Consider selling your dress after the wedding to recover some of the cost.

◆ Consider simple designs without embroidery. Machine work instead of hand beading can greatly reduce costs. A simple dress with simple accessories can look very stylish.

◆ Asking a local dressmaker to copy a style of dress in a cutting edge magazine could help save hundreds (and even thousands) of pounds.

FOR THE BRIDESMAIDS

Although the Bride's dress is of prime importance, the Bride will also need to consider the style and colour of her bridesmaids' dresses.

What type of dress would you like?	Traditional	☐
	Modern	☐
Would you prefer your bridesmaids to wear	Two piece (bodice and skirt)	☐
	Dress	☐
What neckline would you like the bridesmaids' dresses to have?	Strapless	☐
	Sweet heart	☐
	Scoop round	☐
	Halter neck	☐
	V neckline	☐
	Off shoulder – V neckline	☐
	Other _____	
What type of sleeves would you like the bridesmaids' dresses to have?	Sleeveless	☐
	Straps	☐
	Cap/short sleeves	☐
	Long sleeves	☐
	Other _____	

What type of skirt would you like the bridesmaids' dresses to have?	Straight	☐
	A line	☐
	Fishtail	☐
	Ball gown/ Full skirt	☐
	Skirt length: _____	

What colour dresses would you like the bridesmaids to have?

Is there a particular fabric you would like your bridesmaids' dresses to be made of?	Silk	☐
	Satin	☐
	Organza	☐
	Chiffon	☐
	Tulle	☐
	Other _____	

Are there any other accessories your bridesmaids will wear?	Tiara	☐
	Jewellery	☐
	Other _____	

You will need to think about the following things too:

1. Although you are the Bride and it is your day, you need to consider whether your bridesmaids will feel comfortable wearing what you decide. One person can look great in a certain colour where as it can make someone else looked drained. As well as the colour, the style is important too. Again, a certain style could look great on a tall person but could be unsuitable for a shorter person.

2. To avoid upsetting any of your bridesmaids, ask them for their input with the dresses and see what they are comfortable wearing. It may be easier to have a colour scheme but to choose a slightly different style for each person so they are happy wearing it. In the end, you want them to smile for your photographs and not to feel awkward all day as they will be on show too.

3. If they are needed at any fittings or shopping sessions give them plenty of warning and book the date in advance. If you can combine this with a leisurely lunch it will give you a chance to relax and will also show your bridesmaids that the wedding is not taking over everything!

4. Strapless and slinky dresses may look great on your grown up bridesmaids but you will also need to think about suitable designs for any younger bridesmaids or flower girls.

Paste scraps of materials and photos here.

Keeping within Budget

If you are trying to keep costs down, it may be a good idea to limit the number of bridesmaids you have but you can also consider some of the following options:

❖ *Many chain stores now supply inexpensive dresses for younger bridesmaids.*
❖ *Consider looking for older bridesmaids' dresses in the evening wear section of department stores.*
❖ *Look for bridesmaids' dresses in the sales in wedding dress shops.*
❖ *If you are able to find a dressmaker to make your wedding dress, ask about making the bridesmaids' dresses too.*

ACCESSORIES

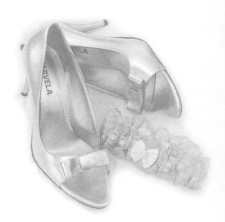

◆ **Shoes**

It is important to look for shoes early on so the Bride can wear them to her dress fittings to ensure the dress length is correct and they are suitable for the style of dress.

Other things to consider are the height of the heel. In particular, if the Bride is a similar height to the Groom, she may want to consider a flatter style so she is not towering over the Groom.

It is also advisable to spend time before the wedding wearing the shoes around the house. On the day they will feel more comfortable and the Bride will be used to walking in them. She will be on her feet for many hours on the wedding day so avoiding blisters and having comfortable shoes is important.

◆ **Jewellery**

The right jewellery can add the finishing touches to the dress. Therefore, it is important to choose jewellery carefully so it complements the outfit and does not overpower it. Jewellery will also need to complement the wedding ring.

It is a good idea to try the jewellery on with the dress (and perhaps on the same day as your hair trial) so that you can see how everything looks altogether. This will give you the opportunity to change anything that is not quite right.

◆ Veil

The Bride can choose whether she would like a veil with her outfit or not. Veils tend to be used more commonly in church weddings.

You will need to decide on the length of veil and order it at the same time as the dress. If you want to have a trial run with your hairstyle, you will need to ensure the veil is ready in time for your trial hair appointment.

◆ **Wrap/Bolero/Cape/Elbow Length Gloves**

Depending on the time of year you get married, you may decide to accessorise your dress with further clothing which can either contribute to the style of your outfit or can help you keep warm. Bridal shops will stock some of these items but many department stores also have ranges of accessories that could enhance your dress and may be a lot cheaper too.

◆ **A Wedding Tradition**

There is a poem 'Something old, something new, something borrowed, something blue' which is reported to date back to Victorian times.

The bride is meant to wear something old to represent her life before she got married, something new to represent her new life with her husband, something borrowed from a bride with a happy marriage for good luck and something blue, the colour of purity and fidelity.

HAIR, MAKE-UP AND NAILS

Every Bride wants to look her best on her wedding day and therefore as well as the clothing and accessories, she will need to consider how she will have her hair on the day.

If the Bride visits a regular hairdressing salon, they may be able to offer a wedding hairstyle package which includes a consultation beforehand, a trial run and then creating the hairstyle on the wedding day. It is important to find someone that the Bride can trust.

At the consultation, the hairdresser should let the Bride know what she will need to bring to the trial. For example, her tiara, her veil or any other accessories she may want to include in the hairstyle, such as flowers.

The trial appointment lets the hairdresser experiment with a number of styles to see which one the Bride is most comfortable with. In particular, if the Bride is considering a drastic change in hairstyle, this is a good time to see if it will work. The Bride may also want to plan a dress fitting on the same day so it is possible to see what the hairstyle looks like with the dress.

When planning the timing of the appointment on the wedding day, the Bride will need to take into consideration the following:

❖ *whether she will need to travel to the hairdresser (and how she will get there and back)*
❖ *whether the hairdresser will come to the place where she is staying*
❖ *whether the hairdresser will have to do bridesmaids' hair as well as her own.*

The Bride will also need to remember to wear clothing that can easily be removed once her hair is done i.e. a button up top rather than a t-shirt that she needs to pull over her head.

Hairdressers will also advise on how to keep the Bride's hair in good condition in the lead up to the wedding. Regular haircuts are important to keep the ends neat.

If the Bride does not want to go to a professional hairdresser, she may want to ask a friend to do her hair or even do her hair herself. Again, trial runs are important to ensure the Bride is happy with her hair.

In terms of make-up, most people are unlikely to have a regular make-up artist in the same way they might have a hairdresser. However, hairdressers may be able to recommend someone if the Bride is considering hiring the services of a professional make-up artist/beautician. Alternatively, it may be possible to ask at make-up counters in a department store whether there are wedding make-up services.

Again, it is important to have a trial run whether the Bride wants to use a professional make-up artist/beautician or ask a friend to do her make-up for her.

Professional make-up artists can also offer advice on skin care before the day.

On the wedding day, the Bride will need to plan her make-up session around the hair session to ensure there is enough time for each.

If the Bride asks a friend to help with hair or make-up, she must be absolutely sure the friend is reliable and can manage the task. She will also need to tell the friend if she does not like something so she that feels her absolute best on her wedding day.

The Bride may also want to invest in a manicure as there may be close up photographs of her hands showing the wedding ring, and of course many people will probably want to see the ring too. As with the hair and make-up it is a good idea to check out possibilities beforehand and have a trial run to make sure the Bride's nails look good on the day.

BRIDE'S ESSENTIAL BAG FOR THE WEDDING DAY

The Bride will not be able to have a handbag with her, therefore it is advisable to prepare a bag of essential items which she can give to a trusted friend or member of her family who will be near by all day. Therefore, if she needs any of the essential items in it, she can still get access to them reasonably easily.

There are a number of items the Bride might require, but as a starting point, here are some suggestions:

❖ *Make-up – including waterproof mascara*
❖ *Tissues*
❖ *Tights/Stockings*
❖ *Headache tablets (and any other medication you may require)*
❖ *Tampons/sanitary towels*
❖ *Small amount of money*
❖ *House key*
❖ *Toothbrush/toothpaste*
❖ *Deodorant/perfume*
❖ *Hairbrush*
❖ *Mirror*
❖ *Hairgrips*

❖ *Phone numbers of suppliers and family members*
❖ *Spare underwear.*

Other essentials you can think of

❖ ....

❖ ....

❖ ....

❖ ....

❖ ....

❖ ....

❖ ....

❖ ....

❖ ....

❖ ....

❖ ....

❖ ....

❖ ....

THE GROOM

Not wanting to outshine the Bride but at the same time wanting to look good on the day to complement her, the Groom will need to decide what to wear too. The checklist below is understandably shorter than the checklist for the Bride's outfit but will give the Groom an idea of different styles of suit jacket available.

It is advisable for the Groom to go and try on different styles and colours to see what suits him best. Unlike the dress, it isn't 'bad luck' for the Bride to see the Groom's outfit before the wedding so the Bride can go along to advise.

Another decision to make is whether to buy or hire. A suit or dinner jacket could be worn again.

Would you prefer	Nehru jacket	☐
	Frock coat	☐
	Morning tail coat	☐
	Dinner jacket	☐
	Highland wear	☐
	Other _____	
What colour suit would you like?	Black	☐
	Grey	☐
	Cream	☐
	White	☐
	Other _____	

What accessories will you require?	Waistcoat	☐
(NB It is a good idea to tie in the	Handkerchief	☐
colour scheme of these with the	Cravat/Tie	☐
colour scheme being used for	Top hat	☐
Bridesmaids' dresses, flowers etc).	Other _____	

Remember to allocate
some time to look for a
wedding ring for the
groom as well as the bride.

THE OTHER MALE ATTENDANTS

The Groom (and the Bride) will need to decide whether to set a general theme (e.g.black tie) which would allow the male attendants to source their own suits or whether they are going to insist that all attendants hire suits of the same style.

If the Bride and Groom are going to pay for the hire, then it will be easier for them to impose the dress code on their attendants. Hire stores may offer a discount if you hire a number of suits from them, for example, four suits for the price of three. In addition, if you hire for a group of attendants the hire store may offer the accessories (such as waistcoats) for a discounted rate or for free.

Traditionally, the Groom pays for the suit hire of the male attendants but they may be happy to pay for their own suit hire. However, it is advisable to discuss this with them at the outset to ensure they are willing to bear the cost. In particular, if the wedding plans involve costly suit hire or the purchase of outfits, the Groom (and his Bride) may want to think about paying for it themselves.

CHAPTER 7

THE WEDDING THEME

3 STEPS TO PLANNING A WEDDING THEME

When planning the theme for your wedding, you have the chance to use all your creativity and produce something that will stay in your memory (and the memories of your guests) for years to come.

If you start thinking about how you want the wedding to look, it is possible to weave the theme throughout the day from your wedding ceremony to the day reception and right through to the evening.

It is often small details that create a very personal effect.

1. **Find Inspiration**
   Starting with a blank canvas can sometimes be more daunting than already having an idea, but it could help to create something unique. Spend time looking at wedding magazines and searching the internet for ideas. The central theme could be based around:

   ❖ *A colour e.g. chocolate and cream*
   ❖ *A flower e.g. red rose*
   ❖ *A place e.g. Paris*
   ❖ *A book*
   ❖ *A season e.g. Autumn.*

Area	Ideas	Example
Colour theme		
Stationery		
Flowers		
Cake		
Decorations		
Music		
Other items		

2. **Gather Ideas based around your Theme**
   Create a mood board based around your theme. Using the internet and/or wedding magazines, you will be able to search for and gather pictures of items that go with your theme to build up a bank of ideas. Your mood board does not just have to be limited to pictures. Samples of ribbon or fabric could be added.

3. **Plan your Theme**
   The theme should be present throughout all areas of your wedding. The grid on page 127 should help you to clarify your ideas.

When choosing a colour theme, keep the venue in mind to make sure the colour will suit the surroundings.

Remember that the theme can extend to any part of your wedding, for example the food. So perhaps if you were to have a December wedding, a menu with turkey and cranberry sauce may be suitable. A wedding with an Italian feel could have a menu with pasta.

Bride

White Chocolate Cheesecake
surrounded by a Dark Chocolate Sauce

Coffee and Sweetmeats

CHAPTER 8

STATIONERY

Wedding stationery will be a key feature of your theme and as invitations are sent out before the wedding, they will set the scene for your big day.

This quick checklist should help you to clarify the type of stationery you will want to source.

What style of stationery would you like?

Hand made	☐
Printed/personalised	☐
Pre-printed/shop bought	☐
Other _____	

What colour scheme would you like for your stationery?

What type of design would you like for your stationery?

By visiting card shops or looking at card websites on the internet, you will be able to look at different options for your wedding stationery. Internet suppliers may even send you samples which can be useful as photos on websites may not always give you a clear enough representation of what the actual product looks like.

Wedding stationery is an area where it is possible to save a lot of money from your budget so it is worth considering whether you have the time to make or print the stationery yourselves. If you feel confident about doing this, you could save up to 75% of the stationery costs by buying the raw materials and assembling them into your invitations, order of service, menu cards and thank you cards.

BUDGET

	Number required	Option A		Option B		Option C	
		Price per item	Total cost	Price per item	Total cost	Price per item	Total cost
Keep the Date Free cards*							
Invitations*							
Order of Service							
Name cards*							
Menu cards							
Thank you Cards*							
Other							

* Allow a few extra for handwriting mistakes!

Have the following details which need to be included been organised?

❖ *Date of wedding*
❖ *Place of marriage*
❖ *Time of marriage*
❖ *Venue for day reception*
❖ *Time for day reception*
❖ *Venue for evening reception*
❖ *Time for evening reception*

Some suppliers of wedding stationery will also be able to offer a seating plan in the same theme as the rest of your stationery. Therefore, it is a good idea to enquire at the outset whether this is an option.

If you are making the stationery yourself, it is also a good idea to consider how you are going to make a seating plan as well as deciding on how many you will need to display at the venue. If you have a large number of guests, you may need several seating plans to avoid everyone crowding around the same one. Also, consider carefully the size of the plan so it is easy for everyone to see and read.

QUESTIONS FOR THE PRINTER

If you do decide to have your invitations printed for you, here are some of the things you may want to consider asking the printer.

Can you print

Keep the date free cards ☐

Invitations ☐

Order of Service ☐

Name cards ☐

Menu cards ☐

Thank you cards ☐

Seating plan ☐

Other _____

Can you show us a mock-up of what the invitation will look like?

Do we get to give final approval before print?

Is there a minimum order quantity?

What is the price for the order?

     Keep the date free cards   £_____

     Invitations   £_____

     Order of Service   £_____

     Name cards   £_____

     Menu cards   £_____

     Thank you cards   £_____

     Seating plan   £_____

     Other _____   £_____

(Deposit/Instalments/Final Payment)

If we need an additional print run, is this possible?

What would be the cost of this?

How long will the printing take?

Is delivery included in the price?

OTHER IDEAS

◆ If you are interested in handmade invitations, find a design that
you like and then copy it. Supplies of card, paper, ribbon, glitter
and other accessories can be bought from most craft paper
shops. Independent shops may also offer advice or short classes
on craft techniques, making it possible for you to create the
wedding stationery yourself. Using a computer, it is also
possible to create and print your own wording for the inside of
the card.

◆ If you do not have the time or inclination to make your own
handcrafted cards, perhaps you can design something suitable
on the computer and print it. Look around for ideas in
magazines and in craft paper shops. Creating something simple
can still look very elegant and effective. For example, your
invitation can be typed and printed on cream paper but if you
add a small amount of confetti into the envelope, the wedding
theme will still be set when the invitation arrives.

◆ Standard design invitations are available at many stationery
and card shops. These are usually sold in packets of 10 or 15 and
will have standard text inside with blank spaces to fill in
appropriate details. This is likely to be a cheaper option
compared to hand-made or printed invitations but has the
drawback of being mass produced and therefore not unique for
your wedding.

◆ More recently, with advances in technology, another option is to send out invitations by email, which saves on printing costs. However, you would need to decide whether this option would work for you and your guests as some people still do not have access to email.

Sample Text for Invitations

Below are a few suggestions for possible text to be included on your invitations. However, it is up to you to decide how you prefer the text to be set out and what you would like the invitation to say. If your family circumstances do not conform to the suggestions below, the internet is a good source of information for alternative suggestions on how best to draft your invitations.

When you are ready to send out your invitations, if you have created a list all the names of guests you are inviting as suggested in chapter 2, you will be able to use this for addressing the invitations and also for recording the responses in your table/spreadsheet as you receive them. This will also make it easier for you to follow up any guests who have not responded to you by the 'reply by' date.

◆ **Suggestion for invitation to day and evening reception**

Mr and Mrs Michael Myers
request the pleasure of your company
(or: request the honour of your presence) at the marriage of their daughter

Elizabeth
to
Mr Jonathan Frost

at
St Mary's Church, Littletown
on Saturday 3rd November 20XX
at 3pm

and afterwards at their reception at

The Castle Hotel, Littletown

Evening reception and buffet to follow from 7pm onwards.

R.S.V.P.

36, Main Street
Big town
XXX XXX
Please reply by 31st August 20XX

◆ **Alternative Suggestion**

Jonathan Frost and Elizabeth Myers
request the pleasure of the company of

....

at their marriage at
on Saturday 3rd November 20XX
The Castle Hotel, Littletown

at 3pm
and afterwards at their sit-down reception at the same venue.

Evening reception and buffet to follow from 7pm onwards.

RSVP
Jonathan Frost and Elizabeth Myers
16 Buttercup Way
Littletown, XXX XXX
Tel: xxxxx xxx xxx
Please reply by 31st August 2007

◆ **Suggestion for evening reception invitation (with invite to wedding ceremony)**

Mr and Mrs Michael Myers
request the pleasure of the company of

....

at the marriage of their daughter

Elizabeth
to
Mr Jonathan Frost

at
St Mary's Church, Littletown
on Saturday 3rd November 20XX
at 3pm

You are requested to return later to attend
the evening wedding reception and buffet

at

The Castle Hotel, Littletown
on Saturday 3rd November 20XX
from 7pm onwards

R.S.V.P.
36, Main Street
Big town
XXX XXX
Please reply by 31st August 20XX

◆ **Suggestion for evening reception invitation**

Mr and Mrs Michael Myers
request the pleasure of the company of

....

at the evening wedding reception and buffet
to celebrate the marriage of their daughter

Elizabeth
to
Mr Jonathan Frost

at

The Castle Hotel, Littletown
on Saturday 3rd November 20XX
from 7pm onwards

R.S.V.P.
36, Main Street
Big town
XXX XXX
Please reply by 31st August 20XX

OTHER THINGS YOU MAY WANT TO INCLUDE WITH YOUR INVITATIONS

As well as the design and the important information such as the date and time of your wedding and wedding reception, there are a number of other pieces of information, you may want to include with your invitation:

◆ **Gift List**
Deciding whether or not to have a gift list is a very personal choice for each Bride and Groom. However, if you are considering this, it will need to be organised before you send out your invitations. If you decide against a gift list and do not want guests to pay for presents, it may be a good idea to include 'No gifts please' on the invitations.

There is now a wide variety of gift lists available on the internet. These include eco-friendly gift lists where all the items sourced are environmentally friendly either through efficient use of energy in production, or through being produced from sustainable materials or made locally to reduce transportation. There are also a number of charity gift lists where, instead of the Bride and Groom receiving gifts, the guests can donate to a charity selected by the Bride and Groom.

Gift lists were traditionally a way of the Bride and Groom receiving all the items they might need to set up a house together. However, in present times people are waiting until they are older to get married, there are also second time round marriages and many couples already live together before the wedding, therefore traditional gift lists are becoming less popular.

Some couples opt for more unusual gift lists where guests can contribute towards holidays or weekends away or perhaps even towards the cost of the wedding photograph album.

◆ **Menu options**

If your catering option requires quests to choose what they would like to eat beforehand, you will need to include this with the invitation, to avoid having to call all your guests up. It may be possible for you or the caterer to create a simple reply form to make it easy for your guests to respond.

Reply Slip

Name of guest: ....

Thank you for the invitation to your day reception

☐   I am able to attend the day reception
☐   I am unable to attend

My choices from the menu for the day reception are:

Starter
☐   Farmhouse Paté & Toast
☐   Char-grilled Vegetable Terrine

Main Course
☐   Farmhouse Grill
☐   Brie & Broccoli Pastry Parcel

Dessert
☐   Apple Pie with Cream/Custard

Please return this slip to
Elizabeth Myers & Jonathan Frost
16 Buttercup Way
Littletown
XXX XXX

Please reply by 31st August 20XX

◆ **Dietary requirements**

Even if your guests do not need to pre-order food, it is a good idea to ask guests to inform you of any allergies or food requirements they may have. If you pass this information onto your caterers, it will enable them to make the necessary arrangements to cater for your guests' dietary requirements whilst at the same time reducing the risk of any claims against you or the caterers.

◆ **Directions/maps**

If many of your guests are travelling from out-of-town, it may be useful for you to provide them with some directions for the wedding ceremony venue and the reception venue. Alternatively, you could mention on your invitation that if they require directions, to contact you.

◆ **Accommodation**

If many of your guests are travelling from out-of-town, you could help them by supplying contact details of local hotels or guest houses that are near (or at) the reception venue. An idea of price per night would also be helpful.

◆ **Programme**

Wedding invitations are notoriously vague when it comes to the programme for the day and when guests can expect to eat. It may be useful to consider including some information with the invitation so guests know what will be happening during the day and also what type of food (finger buffet or 3 course dinner) will be served and when. Here is an example of a programme to show what information you may want to include.

The Marriage of
Elizabeth Myers and Jonathan Frost
3rd November 20XX
Information for Guests

Plan for the day

15.00	Wedding
16.00	Photos at Church
16.30	Depart for wedding reception
17.00	Drinks reception and time for guests to check into accommodation
18.00	Guests to be seated for 3 course meal
20.00	Speeches
20.30	Disco
00.30	Close

Wedding Ceremony

The wedding ceremony is being held at St Mary's Church which is in the centre of Littletown. There is some car parking space in the village car park behind the post office. Please contact us if you require directions.

Wedding Reception

Our reception is being held after the ceremony at the The Castle Hotel in Littletown. Parking at the reception will be sign posted. Please contact us if you need us to send you directions.

Food

At our reception there will be a 3 course meal. When you reply to the invitation, please could you let us know if you would prefer a vegetarian meal. Please also let us know if you have any specific allergies that the caterers should be made aware of.

Accommodation

There is some overnight accommodation available at the reception venue and there are also several other hotels and guest houses nearby. We have block booked all the rooms at the reception venue and will allocate these to guests who would like to reserve them on a first come first serve basis. If all the rooms have been allocated and you require overnight accommodation we will be able to give you a list of other options.

Dress Code

The dress code for the wedding is BlackTie/Formal.

Confetti

The church and reception venue has asked if you could only use bio-degradable confetti.

Gifts

We have decided not to have a traditional gift list.

Contact Details

If you have any questions about the wedding or need directions or accommodation details, we can be contacted in the following ways:

Home telephone:	XXXX XXX XXX
Jon Mobile:	XXXX XXX XXXX
Liz Mobile:	XXXX XXX XXXX
Email:	XXXX XXX XXXX

Here are some examples of the form of words for other items of
stationery that you may want to have printed or create yourself.
The first example shown is not type set for printing. It shows the
correct order of proceedings.

The second example shows how the text would need to be laid
out in order to print doubled sided onto A4. The A4 sheet could
then be folded in half to produce an A5 booklet.

◆ Order of Service – Example One

The Marriage of

Elizabeth Catherine Myers
to
Jonathan Peter Frost

3.00p.m.

St. Mary's Church, Littletown,
Saturday 3rd November 20XX

Entrance of the Bride
Canon in D ....*Pachelbel*

HYMN

Make me a channel of your peace
Where there is hatred let me bring your love
Where there is injury, your pardon, Lord
And where there's doubt, true faith in you
Oh, Master, grant that I may never seek
So much to be consoled as to console;
To be understood as to understand
To be loved, as to love with all my soul.
Make me a channel of your peace
Where there's despair in life let me bring hope;
Where the is darkness, only light;
And where there's sadness, ever joy
Make me a channel of your peace
It is pardoning that we are pardoned
In giving to all men that we receive;
And in dying that we're born to eternal life.

THE MARRIAGE

READING 1 - I will be there – Steven Curtis Chapman
READING 2 - Two are better than one – Ecclesiastes 4:9-12

SERMON

PRAYERS

HYMN

O Lord my God, when I in awesome wonder
Consider all the works Thy hands have made.
I see the stars, I hear the rolling thunder,
Thy pow'r thru-out the universe displayed!

Then sings my soul, my Savior God to Thee:
How great Thou art, how great Thou art!
Then sings my soul,my Savior God to Thee:
How great Thou art, how great Thou art!

When thru the woods and forest glades I wander
And hear the birds sing sweetly in the trees,
When I look down from lofty mountain grandeur
And hear the brook and feel the gentle breeze,

And when I think that God, His Son not sparing,
Sent Him to die, I scarce can take it in
That on the cross, my burden gladly bearing,
He bled and died to take away my sin!

When Christ shall come with shout of acclamation
And take me home, what joy shall fill my heart!
Then I shall bow in humble adoration
And there proclaim, my God how great Thou art!

THE SIGNING OF THE REGISTER

Ave Maria ....Schubert

Exit
Ode to Joy ....Beethoven

◆ Order of Service – Example Two

THE SIGNING OF THE REGISTER

Ave Maria ....Schubert

Exit

Ode to Joy ....Beethoven

The Marriage of

Elizabeth Catherine Myers
to
Jonathan Peter Frost

3.00p.m.

St. Mary's Church, Littletown,
Saturday 3rd November 20XX

Entrance of the Bride
Canon in D ....Pachelbel

HYMN

Make me a channel of your peace
Where there is hatred let me bring your love
Where there is injury, your pardon, Lord
And where there's doubt, true faith in you
Oh, Master, grant that I may never seek
So much to be consoled as to console;
To be understood as to understand
To be loved, as to love with all my soul.
Make me a channel of your peace
Where there's despair in life let me bring hope;
Where the is darkness, only light;
And where there's sadness, ever joy
Make me a channel of your peace
It is pardoning that we are pardoned
In giving to all men that we receive;
And in dying that we're born to eternal life.

THE MARRIAGE

READING 1 - I will be there – Steven Curtis Chapman
READING 2 - Two are better than one – Ecclesiastes 4:9-12

SERMON

PRAYERS

HYMN

O Lord my God, when I in awesome wonder
Consider all the works Thy hands have made.
I see the stars, I hear the rolling thunder,
Thy pow'r thru-out the universe displayed!

Then sings my soul, my Savior God to Thee:
How great Thou art, how great Thou art!
Then sings my soul, my Savior God to Thee:
How great Thou art, how great Thou art!

When thru the woods and forest glades I wander
And hear the birds sing sweetly in the trees,
When I look down from lofty mountain grandeur
And hear the brook and feel the gentle breeze,

And when I think that God, His Son not sparing,
Sent Him to die, I scarce can take it in
That on the cross, my burden gladly bearing,
He bled and died to take away my sin!

When Christ shall come with shout of acclamation
And take me home, what joy shall fill my heart!
Then I shall bow in humble adoration
And there proclaim, my God how great Thou art!

◆ **Order of Ceremony (Civil Ceremony)**

Elizabeth & Jonathan

*Welcome all our guests to our
Civil Ceremony*

The Castle Hotel, Littletown

3rd November 20XX

Arrival of the Bride to.....
The Arrival of the Queen of Sheba - Handel

Welcome

Reading 1
I will be there – Steven Curtis Chapman

Marriage Ceremony

Reading 2
I Wanna Be Yours – John Cooper Clarke

Signing of the Register
Canon in D ....Pachelbel

Reading 3
Eskimo Love Song – Traditional Eskimo

Departure of the Bride and Groom to
The Grand March from Aida

◆ Menu Card

Elizabeth & Jonathan Frost
welcome all their guests
to celebrate their marriage on
Saturday 3rd November 20XX

Programme

5.00pm – Drinks Reception

6.00pm – Guests seated

Dinner served

Speeches and Toast

followed by Disco

12.30am – Disco finishes

Menu

Farmhouse Paté
Vegetarian Option: Char-grilled Vegetable Terrine

Farmhouse Grill
Served with Hot New Potatoes
& Salad Buffet

Vegetarian Option: Brie & Broccoli Pastry Parcel

Country Apple Pie
Served with Cream or Custard

Tea/Coffee

Please note the vegetarian options are only available
for those guests who requested them beforehand.

If you have any other allergies,
please inform the staff at the venue.

CHAPTER 9

DECORATIONS

In the early stages of planning the theme for your wedding, you may have used the grid at the beginning of chapter 7 to think of ideas. However, you will then need to consider everything in more detail so you can source all your requirements, meet your budget and work out who is going to assemble the decorations and when.

	Description	Supplier	Price per unit	Number required	Total price
Confetti on tables					
Wedding favours					
Coloured napkins/serviettes					
Ribbons on napkins/serviettes					
Table Centrepiece					
Flowers					
Balloons					

	Description	Supplier	Price per unit	Number required	Total price
Candles/Tealights /Lights					
Draped fabric					
Miscellaneous (Bubbles, sweets, disposable cameras)					

IDEAS FOR DECORATIONS

Options for decorating your tables and ceremony and reception venues are so varied. The only limitation is your imagination (and also any limits imposed by the venue manager).

Again, using the internet and wedding magazines, it is possible to get endless ideas. Some bridal websites also have forums where brides-to-be can swap ideas. This has the added advantage of talking to other brides who may be more enthusiastic than your single friends about all things wedding related as it applies to them too.

Here are some ideas ranging from very simple to more complex but this is only the starting point....

◆ **Confetti**
It is thought that the tradition of throwing confetti at weddings may have evolved from pagan traditions where wedding guests scattered leaves and flower petals over the Bride and Groom to lead the couple to a happy life with many children.

However, more recently, it has been possible to select many different options for confetti such as metallic hearts or stars, tissue paper hearts or dried rose petals (although these tend to be a more expensive option).

If you plan to use confetti on your tables at your reception, you will need to make sure the venue is happy with your choice. Some venues will only allow bio-degradable confetti or may not allow it at all, if they feel it is too difficult to clear up.

Confetti scattered on tables is a very cost effective way to decorate. Another idea is to include some in your invitations to set the theme from the start.

◆ **Wedding Favours**
It is thought that the tradition of giving favours to guests for special occasions such as at a wedding dates back over a thousand years.

Formerly, the Bride and Groom used to give each guest five sugared almonds to signify: Health, Wealth, Happiness, Long Life and Fertility.

Wedding favours are still a popular way to give your guests a souvenir of your wedding day. Sweets or chocolates (which now tend to be more popular than almonds) are wrapped in cellophane or netting and tied with a ribbon or they could be presented in a small decorative box. It is also possible to attach a label with the name of the Bride and Groom and the date of the wedding.

Wedding favours can be bought ready made or can be made at home for a fraction of the price and the design can be co-ordinated with the design of your invitations and other decorations.

The internet is a good place to source chocolates/sweets for your favours which you can buy in bulk to help keep costs low.

However, as with many wedding related items, new trends have evolved for wedding favours and modern Bride and Grooms now look for new and interesting wedding favours. Examples include:

- *Sourcing sweets that were available when the Bride and Groom were children*
- *Personalised chocolates*
- *Pieces of seaside rock with the Bride and Groom's name through the middle*
- *Miniature bottles of alcohol (you would need to check if the venue would allow this)*
- *Cookies in novelty (wedding related) shapes*
- *Fortune cookies*
- *Lottery tickets*
- *Lottery scratch cards*
- *Packets of seeds that guests can plant (good for a spring wedding)*
- *Small plants in plant pots*
- *Plant Bulbs (Daffodil, Crocus, Tulip)*
- *Novelty soaps (make sure the guest realise these are not edible)*

❖ *Decorative candles*
❖ *Personalised shot glasses*
❖ *Personalised key rings*
❖ *Miniature photo frames*

◆ **Table Centre Piece/Flowers/Balloons**
You may decide that you would like to have a focal point at the centre of your table and options once again are countless.

◆ **Flowers**
Flowers are dealt with separately in Chapter 10.

◆ **Glass Bowl Centrepiece**
Another option is to have a glass bowl at the centre of each table as your focal point.

You could fill these with water and have floating candles in them (but you would need to check regarding fire regulations at the venue).

For a winter wedding, glass bowls filled with pine cones (sprayed silver or gold), holly, mistletoe, and other seasonal decorations such as oranges pierced with cloves could make a very attractive centre piece.

You could fill the bowl with novelty items for your guests such as bubbles, party poppers, feathers, crackers, disposable cameras and sweets.

◆ **Balloon Cluster**

Having a cluster of balloons in the centre of the table can look very pretty and helps to give the room a lift. The balloons are usually tied with coloured ribbon to a decorative weight.

Companies that create balloon clusters will also be able to create other decorations with balloons such as archways.

◆ **Other Options**

For more unusual centrepieces there are other options such as ice sculptures or fruit sculptures. Companies specialising in creating these can be located on the internet. Many show examples of their work on their websites.

You may of course be able to think of other alternatives that will go with your theme. A platter or bowl filled with grapes and cheeses may be appropriate and edible too. A goldfish bowl with live goldfish could be unusual, although you would need to ensure that the welfare of the fish was not compromised by children or other guests.

◆ **Candles/Tea lights**

Some venues will not allow candles/tea lights due to fire regulations. However, for the venues that do, candles/tea lights are a great way to add a magical feel for your evening reception. The key is to use a large number of candles/tealights. Subject to the agreement of the venue manager, tea lights can be distributed on tables, around the finger buffet table and on any flat surface where there is no risk of burning anything.

It is a good idea to check that whichever holders you use for candles/tealights do not get hot and damage any surface they will be placed on. If you are planning to use candles/tealights care must be taken especially if children and babies are present.

Glass lanterns are also available from many homeware shops.

It is possible to buy inexpensive tea light/candle holders from most homewear shops. A cheap and environmentally friendly alternative would be to recycle empty baby food jars which are just as effective.

If it is possible to dim the lights at the reception venue in the evening, the tea lights will provide an atmospheric glow that is bound to be enjoyed by your guests.

If candles and tea lights are not allowed at the venue or you feel that having candles is too risky, it is now possible to source battery-operated tealights. These can be placed inside holders or paper lantern bags and will give the same effect without the use of naked flames.

Always beware of fire risks and take into account unexpected behaviour of guests and children.

◆ **Fairy Lights**

Some venues may already have fairy lights which can be twisted around railings, and wooden beams or in trees.

If your venue does not already have fairy lights but you would like to have them at your reception, you would need to discuss this possibility with the venue manager. There are strict health and safety procedures to follow with electrical items but it may be possible for you to arrange for fairy lights to be assembled for your reception.

Some suppliers are also able to drape the walls of a venue with star cloth (dark cloth with small lights dotted throughout). Again, you would need to discuss the possibility of having this assembled for your reception with the supplier and also with the venue manager to ensure compliance with regulations.

◆ **Draped Fabric**

Another thing to consider is using fabric to add some colour to your reception. Organza can be used on top of white table linen to introduce your colour scheme. Netting can be tied into bows on chair backs. Organza can be pinned into drapes around the top table (or on the front of a stage if the function room has one) and bows can be tied at the top of each drape. (Take into account fire risks mentioned previously).

Although using fabric will add extra expense, it is possible to source cheaper fabric in a number of ways. Some shops sell fabric seconds at a greatly reduced rate. Any imperfections can been hidden within the drapes or just cut out of the fabric. If you are buying fabric in bulk, it is worth asking for a discount.

When you pack up your decorations for the reception venue, label a separate box/bag for each table and place everything you need for each table in the relevant box/bag. When the boxes/bags are taken to the reception venue it will make it so much easier and quicker to lay the right things out on each table.

CHAPTER 10

FLOWERS

Flowers can be a very effective way of creating a visual impact at your wedding.

There are so many options for flower arrangements including bouquets, baskets for the flower girl, buttonholes, corsages, pew ends, pedestal displays in the church, pedestal displays in the reception venue, table centrepieces, top table arrangement and buffet table arrangements.

◆ **Questions for the Bride and Groom**

What colour scheme have you
  decided on for your flowers?

What type of flower would you like to
  have as the main flower in your displays?

- ☐ Rose
- ☐ Gerbera
- ☐ Lily
- ☐ Other _____
- ☐ Would like advice from florist

Which of the following items are essential for your wedding day?

		Quantity
☐	Bridal bouquet	_____
☐	Bridesmaid bouquet	_____
☐	Flower girl basket	_____
☐	Haircomb	_____
☐	Hair circlet	_____

		Quantity
☐	Buttonhole	_____
☐	Corsage	_____
☐	Pew ends	_____
☐	Pedestal arrangements	_____
☐	Top table arrangement	_____
☐	Buffet table arrangement	_____
☐	Table centrepiece	_____
☐	Gift bouquets	_____

Which of the following items are desirable (but not essential) for your wedding day?

		Quantity
☐	Bridal bouquet	_____
☐	Bridesmaid bouquet	_____
☐	Flower girl basket	_____
☐	Haircomb	_____
☐	Hair circlet	_____
☐	Buttonhole	_____
☐	Corsage	_____
☐	Pew ends	_____
☐	Pedestal arrangements	_____
☐	Top table arrangement	_____
☐	Buffet table arrangement	_____
☐	Table centrepiece	_____
☐	Gift bouquets	_____

WORKING WITH YOUR FLORIST

There are many suppliers you may decide to use who may not have a business premises for you to visit (e.g. photographer) and therefore you will need to rely on their marketing material, personal contact and references to decide if they are going to provide the level of service you require. However, many florists operate from a shop which gives you the advantage of going in to have a look at where they work and see some of the arrangements they have created. They should also have a portfolio of previous work for you to browse before you make up your mind as to which florist to choose.

Flowers for your wedding can appear expensive but when you understand more about the role the florist has to play in creating your arrangements, it is easier to see where the cost comes from.

The florist has to spend time with you discussing your requirements to gain an understanding of what you are looking for as well as the budget you have in mind. They then have to use their imagination to create a design that will be to your taste and will also fit in with your ideas.

The flowers need to be ordered in the correct quantities to arrive at the right time so they are in full bloom on the right day (and have not gone past their best). The flowers need to be conditioned and stored so that they do not wilt. This is particularly important in hot summer months.

The florist will then only be able to prepare the arrangements the day before the wedding which often involves working late in the night to get everything done.

Finally, the flowers will need to be delivered to the various locations where they are required (Bride's house, church, reception venue).

If cost is a pressing issue, by considering carefully how you use flowers at your wedding reception it is possible to reduce the amount you spend without compromising the overall visual impact for your guests or for the photographs.

❖ *Consult your florist to see which flowers would be in season on your wedding day and see if these would be cheaper.*
❖ *Ask your florist about floral arrangement designs that incorporate a few stunning flowers surrounded by green foliage. Foliage tends to be a lot cheaper than the flowers.*
❖ *A hand-tied bouquet tends to be cheaper than a shower or trailing bouquet.*

❖ *If you are having pew ends at the church, consider alternating floral arrangements with ribbons so that you need fewer floral arrangements.*

❖ *At the reception consider having a single flower in a vase as a centrepiece rather than an arrangement. Or as described in the decorations section, replace flowers with an alternative centrepiece.*

If you decide on the number and types of arrangements you require and decide how much money you can afford to spend, your florist may then try to work out a design that will be achievable within that budget.

Take a fabric sample from the Bridesmaids' dresses with you to the florist as this will help the florist to choose appropriate flowers. Also, give the florist details of how tall each Bridesmaid is, as this will help to decide on the design of the bouquets etc.

Once the florist has given you the first quote, it may be possible for you to reduce the price by asking about alternative possibilities such as using different flowers, reducing the size of your arrangements etc.

You will also need to check that price includes delivery and give details of each location e.g. Bride's house, church/civil ceremony location, reception. Provide a contact name or number for each location so the florist has someone they can call if there is a problem, e.g. they have difficulty finding the place.

Also include a timetable of when the flowers need to be at each location. For example, the Bride will need her bouquet much earlier in the day than the reception venue will need its table centrepieces.

CHAPTER 11

OTHER IDEAS FOR ENTERTAINING THE WEDDING GUESTS

As well as decorating the reception and making it look wonderful for your guests, you may want to consider other ideas to entertain your guests and also make your reception unique by giving it a personal touch.

Here are some ideas to get you started and may lead to developing others suitable for your reception:

1. **Chocolate Fountain**
   These have recently become very popular at weddings and give your guests a chance to dip pieces of fruit and other delicious treats into flowing warm chocolate. They are available for hire and now it is even possible to buy smaller versions. Chocolate fountains are often a magnet for wedding guests but beware that the chocolate can get everywhere and if you are particularly worried about having chocolate marks on your wedding dress, this may not be an option for you. You may want to think about having a member of the catering staff supervise the use of the chocolate fountain to avoid such disasters!

2. **Photography**
   In addition to your official wedding photographs, advances in technology now mean there are other ways to capture images

from the day. Disposable cameras on tables are a cheap way to get a large amount of extra snaps of your guests. If you put out signs to remind people to use them and also make announcements during the speeches, you are more likely to get people to take photographs.

Another alternative is to have a Polaroid camera positioned somewhere at the reception venue and ask guests to take pictures of each other and then put them up on a wall or notice board (with permission of the venue). A variation on this would be to buy or borrow a digital printer for the day and print photographs off that have been taken using a digital camera. You may need to draft in couple of helpers to take responsibility for this or there are professional companies that will do this for a fee.

3. Video Diary

You may decide to have a professional wedding video taken on the day but it might be interesting to set up a video camera at your wedding reception so guests can come and record messages throughout the day in the style of a reality tv video diary. This could capture some very funny moments but also give guests a chance to leave a personal message.

4. Karaoke

For people who love to sing and be the centre of attention, a karaoke section during your reception could liven things up. Remember that some guests may not enjoy singing though, so it is important not to pressurise people to take part so they do not feel uncomfortable.

5. **Children's Activities**

If you are considering having children at your reception, you may want to put some thought into providing some activities for them. Although they may be happy to dance at the disco, the day can be very long and boring for younger guests (especially during the speeches).

- ❖ *Activity packs including colouring books and coloured pencils are a good way to keep children happy and quiet. It is possible to put an activity pack together, or some internet based companies supply ready assembled packs for boys and girls of different age ranges with appropriate toys and activities for each.*
- ❖ *Packs of cards or question and answers quiz game cards are a good idea for the reception tables and adults can join in too.*
- ❖ *It is possible to hire the services of a children's entertainer, which could include supervision of crafts for children or activities such as face painting.*
- ❖ *Another alternative is to ask some of your guests to organise some games for children which could include a treasure hunt, some races or some party games such as musical statues if the disco is set up a little earlier.*

❖ *It may be possible to hire a magician to perform tricks for your guests, which could be another good way to keep your younger guests occupied.*

6. Guest Book

Having a book that your guests can sign and write messages in has become popular and ends up being a keepsake for the Bride and Groom. If you do not want your guest to write standard messages, give them some ideas or topics that you would like them to write about e.g. how they know you, where they met you, funny stories from the past etc.

7. Ice Breakers for Guests

It can be difficult for your guests if they are sitting at a table with people they do not know or if they don't know anyone at the wedding. It may help them if you can give them some introductions to the other people on their table. If you write a couple of sentences about each of your guests and place a card on the table that explains who everyone is on that table, your guests will be able to read about each other. It will also give you a chance to say something nice about each person.

You may decide it would be good for all your guests to read about each other so if you display all the descriptions of all your guests on a wall or a board (with the venue's permission) it could be a point of interest.

8. More Unusual Ideas

Some couples like the idea of releasing doves at their wedding. There are companies that will supply doves in cages together with a trained handler to ensure safe release. The doves are homing birds so will find their way back.

It is now also possible to release butterflies. There are companies who will supply them either in individual boxes so all guests can release one or in a box for a mass release.

However, it is important to think about whether your guests will appreciate this. Some people may have phobias of birds or butterflies. There are also practicalities involved for example, the doves and the butterflies can only be released in certain weather conditions.

These are just a few ideas but with a bit of imagination, I am sure there are many more options for making your reception unique.

Some of these ideas are very simple and can be organised before the day, however, others may need supervision. Therefore, you will need to either buy in the services of a professional to take control and organise the activity or you will need to give the responsibility to one of your friends or family members. You will need to brief the person fully on what you expect them to do.

CHAPTER 12

OTHER ARRANGEMENTS

HEN AND STAG PARTY

One of the traditions associated with getting married is the celebration of 'one last night of freedom' through holding a stag party for the Groom and a hen party for the Bride.

The organisation of the stag and hen parties is usually the responsibility of the Best Man and Chief Bridesmaid but the Bride and Groom may decide it is easier to organise these themselves. If they have a circle of friends drawn from different areas of their lives (childhood, college/university, work, different areas they have lived in) it may be easier for them to be the main organiser.

In most cases, the stags and hens all pay for themselves on the stag or hen party, therefore it is important to find out early on what amount everyone can afford to pay.

◆ **Questions for the Organiser of the Hen Party**

What is the total budget per person
for the hen night?   £_____

What is the location for the hen night?

At home	☐
Local	☐
Other City	☐
Outside UK	☐

What activities will you want to take part in on the hen night?

Spa/Beauty	☐
Pub Crawl	☐
Meal Out	☐
Nightclub	☐
Karaoke	☐
Other _____	☐

What are the costs per person?

Activity	£_____
Drinks	£_____
Food	£_____
Nightclub entrance	£_____
Transport	£_____
Accommodation	£_____
Clothing e.g. printed t-shirts	£_____
Other _____	£_____

◆ **Questions for the Organiser of the Stag Party**

What is the budget per person
for the stag night?   £ _____

What is the location for the stag night?

At home	☐
Local	☐
Other City	☐
Outside UK	☐

What activities will you want to take part in on the stag night?

Watching Football	☐
Go karting	☐
Paintballing	☐
Pub crawl	☐
Meal Out	☐
Nightclub	☐
Karaoke	☐
Other _____	☐

What are the costs per person?

Activity	£_____
Drinks	£_____
Food	£_____
Nightclub entrance	£_____
Transport	£_____
Accommodation	£_____
Clothing e.g. printed t-shirts	£_____
Other _____	£_____

7 STEPS TO PLANNING A STAG/HEN PARTY

Once you have thought about what you might want to do for the stag or hen party use the following steps to help you plan the event.

If you decide to go on a pub crawl in your local town, the amount of organisation involved will be far less than if you decide to go abroad for several days, so the steps need to be adapted accordingly.

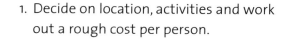

1. Decide on location, activities and work out a rough cost per person.

2. Write to all the people you want to invite asking them to keep the proposed date of the stag/hen party free and telling them what you plan to do and roughly how much you expect it to cost. Give them a deadline by which to reply.

3. Keep a list of everyone who has responded and chase up people who haven't replied by the deadline.

4. Send a letter to each person who has agreed to come telling them how much they need to pay and give them a date by which they should send the money.

5. Make a provisional booking for:
   An activity (if necessary)
   Overnight accommodation (if necessary)
   Transport (if necessary)
   Find out what the procedure is for group bookings, payment terms and cancellations. It is important to do this in advance as you will need to collect money from all the attendees and you do not want to be left with a large bill if anyone does not pay you or if they decide not to attend.

6. Confirm the bookings and ensure payments are made.

7. Inform everyone of arrangements, where to meet, what time etc. If you are flying abroad, remind everyone they will need a valid passport and travel insurance.

KEEPING WITHIN BUDGET

The costs for a hen/stag party can soon add up when you start to take food, alcohol, accommodation, transport and any other leisure activities into account. The introduction of low-cost flights, has made it easier for people to hold hen and stag weekends in European cities, but it can increase the cost of the occasion to several hundred pounds per person.

With some careful planning and a bit of creativity it is possible to have hen and stag nights which are unforgettable but do not cost a fortune at a time when funds are likely to be stretched.

◆ Think local – going to another city or abroad involves transport costs and possibly overnight accommodation. If you choose to do something nearer to home, it will save cash. If your friends live locally it will not break the bank for them too.

◆ Rather than going out, think about a stag/hen/hag (combined stag and hen) party at home. If your guests all bring a bottle, there should not be too many other costs involved. There is still a lot of scope to be creative with party games and fancy dress to make it the most talked about event (until your wedding reception!)

◆ Keep it low-key and sophisticated. You might feel that a large stag or hen party is not for you. Perhaps celebrating with a couple of close friends or family members sounds more appealing.

◆ Without wanting to sound negative, another option is to decide whether you actually want a hen or stag party at all? In particular for the stags, we have all heard of many horror stories of Grooms waking up at the opposite end of the country or finding themselves chained naked to a lamp post! Of course, a stag or hen party is a great way to get together with all your friends before your wedding day, but it may be worth thinking carefully about whether YOU actually want to take part in the activities of your stag or hen night or do you feel you ought to due to the pressure from your friends.

EXAMPLES OF LETTERS

As with every stage of the wedding planning it is advisable to put everything down in writing in a letter or email, so that everyone is clear about the arrangements and what is expected of them.

◆ **Stag Party Abroad – Letter 1**

Dear All,

It may have come to your attention that Liz has finally relented and agreed to marry me and that she is currently busy trying to organise our wedding for this coming November.

Now I was totally unaware of this but she assures me that it is traditional for the Groom to arrange a trip to mainland Europe for him and an elite number of his friends to celebrate the forthcoming nuptials. Can't say I was particularly bothered but she insists that we go and uphold this wonderful tradition. I have decided on Amsterdam for a long weekend.

So now is the time to get to work on your spouses and employers to obtain a pass for a weekend away.

The plan is to depart on the afternoon of the 6th September and to return (hopefully with the same number of people as we went out with) on the 9th September.

At the moment flights are reasonably cheap and we can get them for about £70, however the price will probably go up pretty quickly so I need to know whether you can make it as soon as possible so that I can get them booked.

To confirm your place, text me as soon as you can on XXXXX XXX XXX and I will book the flights. I need to know by March 9th at the very latest.

I hope to get the flights and hotel booked for just over £200, so the hotel may not be 5 star but I have a feeling other than a few hours sleep it won't be used much.

So if you fancy a weekend away you please forward me a cheque for £50 to act as a deposit (and to ease the strain on my credit card from booking the flights) along with your email address.

I will confirm when the flights are booked and will start looking for hotels. I'm thinking if I ask for the cash in instalments then it's easier on you all.

I really hope you will be able to come but I know we all have busy lives and responsibilities so will understand if you can't make it.

Look forward to hearing from you!

Jon

◆ **Stag Party Abroad – Letter 2 (follow up to letter 1)**

Dear all,

Less then 3 weeks till the stag!

I thought it was time to give you a few more details so that you all know where you need to be and when.

Flight times:

Outward – Flight number 5477 - Thursday 6th September 15.50, arrive in Amsterdam at 18.05 (local time)

Return – Flight number 5478 -Sunday 9th September 16.30, arrive at Big Town Airport 16.45 (local time)

You will need the flight number to be able to check in. Suggested check in is 2 hours before departure, the gate closes at 15.20. If you are late then we will go without you, not my rules but the airport's!

General consensus is hand luggage only as it will save time waiting for lost luggage at the other end and wearing the same clothes for 3 days.

Please remember the new security details around hand luggage and liquids.

Can we all ask to try and get seats on rows 10,11,12,13 as this way we might all end up in the same part of the plane.

May I suggest we meet in the bar in the departures hall through the security gates from 2pm onwards.

We are staying in the Hotel Tulip, the contact details are below in case any of our better halves need us in a emergency:-

Hotel Tulip
Amsterdam
Tel +31 (0) XX XX XXX

Make sure you all have a valid passport and travel insurance.

I think that should just about cover everything, however if you have any queries just give me a call.

See you in the bar!

Jon

◆ Hen Party (Local) – Letter 1

An Invitation
to
Liz's Chick Dinner

Saturday, 29th September 20XX

Dear

As you will now be aware – what with you having received a wedding invitation and all – Jon finally did the decent thing and asked me to marry him! With a wedding planned for November, I am reliably informed that tradition dictates that I arrange a gathering of my closest friends for a night of fine food, exotic cocktails, stimulating conversation and maybe a little dancing.

So, it's an excuse for a new glitzy outfit and a night away from our respective fiancés, husbands, boyfriends, children, jobs, mortgages, pets, housework and whatever that week's reality TV show is.

The date is Saturday 29th September, the venue is the Little Sicily restaurant in Middletown and the plan is a sophisticated evening of early evening cocktails followed by dinner and then rounded off with dancing and possibly (or highly likely) more cocktails!

I really hope you that you will be able to join me in what will be one of my last girly nights out as a singleton before Jon has me locked me away in the kitchen.

Please can you let me know by the 31st August 20XX if you will be able to come.

I can be texted on XXXX XXX XXX or emailed at XXXXXXXXXX. I will then contact you all again to confirm times, menu choices and other arrangements.

Can't wait to see you all!

Liz

◆ Hen Party (Local) – Letter 2 (Follow up to Letter 1)

Liz's Chick Dinner

Saturday, 29th September 20XX

Dear

Thank you for accepting my invitation for a sophisticated night of partying to celebrate my 34th last night of freedom before Jon locks me away under the stairs.

We will be meeting in the upstairs bar at Little Sicily Restaurant on High Street in Middletown at 8pm. Our table will be ready for 9pm, and the starters should be served shortly after. Once we have eaten, the upstairs bar is available for us to continue our frivolities with music and dancing until late.

The restaurant needs us to pre-order food so they don't have to wait around on the night whilst we make up our minds.

I have included the menu for you to look at and make your selection.

Could you please let me know **by the 15thSeptember 20XX** what you would like to eat so that I can get all our choices to the restaurant. Unlike Jon's multiple stag parties, I won't be

---

collecting deposits or setting up monthly payment plans as we can all just pay on the night.

I look forward to seeing you all in your new sparkly dresses that have been bought by our respective other halves to make up for the 3 months' worth of salary some of them have spent on the Amsterdam trip. At least we will know they are all at home either baby sitting or playing taxi for us on the night!

If you have any questions you can get me on XXXX XXX XXX or by email at XXXXXXXXXX

Can't wait to see you all!

Liz

PHOTOGRAPHER

After the wedding reception and catering, photography at your wedding is probably one of the most important items, as you are going to want to capture the memories of your wedding day.

A lot of responsibility lies with the wedding photographer to 'get it right' as once the moment has passed, it is not going to be possible to recapture it. Wedding photographers therefore have to acquire their skill over many years. As well as the actual photography, they also need to be able to organise the guests into appropriate groups and so people management skills are also very important.

Finding the right photographer for you is therefore vital to ensure you are comfortable on the day, your guests are not bossed around too much and you get the photographs you want.

5 Steps to Finding a Photographer

1. **Discuss your requirements for the day**

   How important are the photographs of your wedding for you?

   Where do you want the photographer to take photographs?
   - *At the Bride's house*
   - *Before the wedding ceremony*
   - *During the ceremony*
   - *After the ceremony*
   - *At the reception*

   What style of photographs would you like?
   - Traditional (posed group shots)
   - Reportage (unposed photographs captured by the photographer from the sidelines)

   You will also need to check with the registrar or vicar whether it is acceptable for photographs to be taken during the ceremony.

   And you 'll need to check with the reception venue if it is acceptable for photographs to be taken there.

2. Search

As with all the other items for your wedding day, information gathering and searching for suppliers is an integral part of finding the right photographer for you. As discussed in previous chapters, good sources of information are the internet, local directories, wedding fairs and word of mouth.

Many photographers use their websites to display their work which can help you to see what style they use for the photographs and whether you think this would suit you.

Others will have an information pack that you can ask them to send you and many will supply a CD of photographs so you can view them on your PC. You may also get an idea of their charging structure.

Most photographers will ask you the date of your wedding before giving you any information about their services. If they work alone and can only book one wedding per day, they tend to check first whether they are available on the day before giving you more information on their services.

3. Shortlist

Once you have done your information gathering, shortlist 3 or 4 photographers that have appealed to you the most and arrange to meet them.

Criteria for choosing them could include price (and charging structure), style of photography, presentation of website, recommendations.

The following grid should help you to compare them:

Do you belong to any professional photography associations?

What is your charging structure for the photography? (Deposit/Instalments/Final Payment)

How long will you be taking photographs for?

What type and how many group photos will you take?

Do you do a mix of colour and black & white photographs?

Do you supply...
    Prints
    CD of photos
    Photos displayed on website
    Negatives (if using film photography)
    Are these included in the price or are these priced separately?

How much are reprints?

Do you have any former clients we can contact for a reference?

Can we come and see you at work at a wedding?

Have you taken photographs at the wedding ceremony venue/reception venue before?

What contingency plans do you have in place if something goes wrong beyond your control?

When will we get the photographs/album?

Do you hold public liability/professional indemnity insurance?

Photographer A	Photographer B	Photographer C	Photographer D

As well as asking the above questions to the photographer, the following checklist can be used by the Bride and Groom to record their impressions of the photographers once they meet them.

Would you feel comfortable being photographed by this photographer?
How do they interact with you? Do they seem pushy? Do they listen to your ideas?
Do you like the look of the photographs shown by the photographer of previous weddings they have worked at?
The style The group photographs Photographs of items e.g. bouquets, decorations
Do you like the albums the photographer can offer to display your photographs?
Is there anything you particularly like about them/their work?
Is there anything you dislike about them/their work?

Photographer A	Photographer B	Photographer C	Photographer D

4. Choose your favourite

Once you have met with all your selected photographers, hopefully, you will be able to select one that meets all your needs. If not, search for a few more and meet them until you have found one you are satisfied with.

Make sure you get a confirmation of your booking in writing from the photographer. The confirmation should include all the details of locations, timings etc as well as the cost and the services agreed.

5. And if you're still not sure

Some photographers may offer you the chance to do a pre-wedding photo shoot. This could help you to get to know the photographer better and make you feel more relaxed about having your photographs taken on the day. It could also help the photographer find out more about what you want.

Keeping within Budget

Wedding photography is one of the most difficult areas in which to save money as there is usually so much importance attached to wedding photographs. Here are some ideas to keep costs down with wedding photography. However, even if you book a more expensive photographer, you may want to supplement the main photographs with some of these ideas.

Here are a few ideas on how to get the best deal:

◆ Start searching for your wedding photographer very early. Wedding photographers get booked up many months in advance and if your wedding is only a couple of months away you are very unlikely to be able to negotiate a better price for your photography package. Ask all your family members, friends and colleagues to see if anyone can recommend a good photographer from their own experiences of any weddings they may have attended recently.

◆ It may be possible for you to choose a basic photography package with your photographer for a lower price, which contains the main photographs you require for the day. You could then supplement this by asking a friend or a member of the family to take more pictures at the same time so you end up with a mixture of 'official' and 'unofficial' photographs. Make sure this person is reliable and confident or ask a couple of people to take on this role.

◆ Search for photographers/photographic companies who do not necessarily specialise in wedding photography. You may be able to find a photographer who makes a living doing other types of photography during the week but might be wiling to photograph your wedding as a one off.

◆ Some companies offer a wedding photography service where you pay per hour for the photographer's time. The photographs are then displayed on the company website so that you and your guests can choose which images you want to buy and download.

◆ Whether you choose to have an official photographer or not, a good way to get lots of photographs is to put out disposable cameras on tables for your guests to take pictures. If you attach a label to each camera with instructions asking guests to use up the film and telling them where to leave the camera at the end of the reception, you can send these off for developing and are likely to get a very varied set of photographs. It is also a good idea to give out verbal reminders about the cameras throughout the reception so that people do not forget to use them. You will also need to let people know where to leave the cameras at the end of the night.

◆ If your photographer charges for their time and for the photograph prints separately, ask them whether they can supply gift vouchers. You could then include these on your gift list if you decide to have one.

VIDEOGRAPHER

You may decide that as well as official wedding photographs, you want a video of your wedding so you can relive the day and see some of the moments you may have missed on the day.

Finding the right videographer for you will be a similar process to finding the correct photographer. The quality and style of the final video as well as feeling comfortable with the person taking the video is important.

5 STEPS TO FINDING A VIDEOGRAPHER

1. **Discuss your requirements for the day**

   Where do you want the videographer to take video footage?
   * *At the Bride's house*
   * *Before the wedding ceremony*
   * *During the ceremony*
   * *After the ceremony*
   * *At the reception*

   What style of video would you like?
   * *Traditional*
   * *Set to music*
   * *Karaoke (a recent trend has been for the Bride and Groom and even their guests to mime to a favourite song in their video)*

You will also need to check with the registrar or vicar whether it is acceptable for video footage to be taken during the ceremony.

And you'll need to check with the reception venue whether it is acceptable for video footage to be taken there.

2. Search

As with photography, the initial step of information gathering is so important in finding the right option for you. Good sources of information are the internet, local directories, wedding fairs and word of mouth.

Videographers should be able to meet with you and present examples of previous videos they have taken at weddings to give you an idea of the quality of the finished product.

Most videographers will ask you the date of your wedding before giving you any information about their services. If they work alone and can only book one wedding per day, they tend to check first whether they are available on the day before giving you more information on their services.

3. Shortlist

Once you have gathered all your information, shortlist 3 or 4 videographers who have appealed to you the most and arrange to meet them.

Criteria for choosing them could include price (and charging structure), style of video, recommendations.

The following grid should help you to compare them.

Do you belong to any professional videography associations?
What is your charging structure for the videography? (Deposit/Instalments/Final Payment)
How long will you be taking video footage for?
How much are further copies of the video?
Do you have any former clients we can contact for a reference?
Can we come and see you at work at a wedding?
Have you taken video footage at the wedding ceremony venue/reception venue before?
What contingency plans do you have in place if something goes wrong beyond your control?
When will we get the video?
Do you hold public liability/professional indemnity insurance? Will you apply for a private function video/DVD licence?

Videographer A	Videographer B	Videographer C	Videographer D

As well as asking the above questions to the videographer, the following checklist can be used by the Bride and Groom to record their impressions of the photographers once they meet them.

Would you feel comfortable being filmed by this videographer?

How do they interact with you? Do they seem pushy?
Do they listen to your ideas?

Do you like the look of the videos of previous weddings they have worked at?

The style
The presentation
The music (if any)

Is there anything you particularly like about them/their work?

Is there anything you dislike about them/their work?

Videographer A	Videographer B	Videographer C	Videographer D

4. Choose your favourite

Once you have met with all your selected videographers, hopefully, you will be able to select one who meets all your needs. If not, search for a few more until you have found one you are satisfied with.

Make sure you get a confirmation of your booking in writing from the videographer. The confirmation should include all the details of locations, timings etc as well as the cost and the services agreed.

Keeping within Budget

If you have a limited budget, it may be that you have to decide to spend money on photography rather than a video. However, you could consider the following options:

◆ Can any of your guests take video footage for you? It may not turn out as a professional piece of work but if you have this in addition to your photographs, you may find it is an extra souvenir of your day.

◆ As mentioned in Chapter 11 (page 179) perhaps you could set up a stationary video camera for your guests to come and record their messages for you. You would not get any formal footage of the ceremony or reception but it would give your guests a chance to say something.

THE WEDDING CAR AND CHAUFFEUR

Although there are the bigger issues to consider such as the venue and catering which take a lot of time and organisation, another important one you will need to look at is travel arrangements for the Bride, Groom and other members of the wedding party.

The Bride is usually going to need to have transport from where she is getting ready to where the ceremony is taking place. The Bride and Groom then need to be taken from the wedding ceremony to the reception.

◆ **Questions for the Bride and Groom**

Is the type of car you have very important to you?

What type of car are you looking for?

Something traditional

Rolls Royce	☐
Vintage	☐
Horse Drawn Carriage	☐
Other _____	

Something modern/quirky

Limousine	☐
Fire Engine	☐
Double Decker Bus	☐
American Cadillac	☐
Other	_____

Which trips does the car need to make?
(e.g. does it need to take the bridesmaids and then come back for the Bride?)

1. _____
_____
2. _____
_____
3. _____
_____

Or, would you need 2
(or more cars) for the trip(s)

Do you need transport for anyone else?
If so, who?

As with previous suppliers, there are a number of ways you can find out what transport is available to hire in your area including, the internet, directories, wedding fairs, wedding magazines and word of mouth. The following grid is designed to help you assess any transport providers you decide to meet with.

Questions for the Chauffeur
What type of car(s)/transport do you have?
Can we come and see the car(s)/transport?
Can you take the bridesmaids first and then come back for the Bride?
Do you have other car(s)/transport available for the Bridesmaids? (If the journey is too lengthy to make 2 trips)
What is the price for hiring the transport for the journeys we require? (Deposit/Instalments/Final Payment)
Do you charge extra if the timetable for the day overruns?
If yes, how much extra?
Do you book more than one wedding per car per day?
What contingency plans do you have in place if something goes wrong beyond your control?
Do you have appropriate insurance cover?
What else do you provide as part of the service? e.g ribbon on car, champagne

Supplier A	Supplier B	Supplier C	Supplier D

KEEPING WITHIN BUDGET

If your budget is tight, you may want to consider how important it is for you to hire an expensive car for what may be a fairly short trip.

Here are some ideas that could work out cheaper for you:

◆ Vintage cars tend to be more expensive than modern cars, so unless this is one of things you have dreamed of to make you wedding day complete, it should be possible to find a cheaper solution.

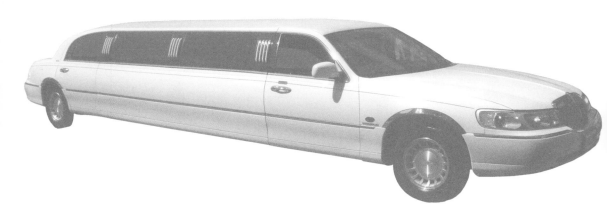

◆ Do you have a family member or a friend with a car that could be used or could they hire a car for the day? (Check insurance cover if considering this option.)

◆ If you are able to arrange your wedding ceremony and your reception at the same location, you could eliminate the need for a car altogether.

◆ Is there anyone who could give the bridesmaids a lift, cutting out the need for a second car?

◆ Or can the chauffeur take the bridesmaids first and then come back to pick up the Bride? This would save the cost of having two cars but does depend on the distances that have to be travelled to ensure it can be done in time.

THE HONEYMOON

This is only a short section on your honeymoon as there are so many options available and it would be impossible to cover them here, but here are a few practical points to think about when planning your honeymoon:

For the Groom
◆ If you are planning to make the honeymoon a surprise, let your Bride know of the type of climate to expect and activities you may be involved in whilst on your honeymoon (e.g. sunbathing, sightseeing). She will then be able to pack appropriate clothing.

Practical Aspects
◆ If the Bride is changing her surname, find out early from the Passport Office or your travel agent when the appropriate time is to do this on her passport.

◆ Check both your passports are valid and in date up to your return date. Some destinations require that you have 6 months left on your passport before its expiry date.

◆ Check what you will require for your destination in terms of visas, identification documents, vaccinations, so that you have enough time to sort these things out before your wedding.

◆ Start gathering clothing items that you want to take a few weeks before your wedding and try to pack 2 weeks beforehand.

With everything else that you will be organising, you can get this done early.

◆ Order your foreign currency early if it is required and organise travel insurance..

Destinations

◆ Choosing your destination may be a difficult decision, as it is now easier to travel than ever before. However, you should consider what holiday activities you both enjoy as it is a chance for you of you to relax after the wedding. For example, if one of you enjoys sunbathing and the other enjoys outdoor pursuits you may be able to find a destination that offers both these options.

◆ If your preferred options are very varied, perhaps you may consider a 2-destination break. For example, travelling to a city for some sightseeing, shopping and nightlife before heading to a beach destination for some relaxation.

◆ You may also consider 2 separate long weekend breaks. Perhaps a few days at a remote cottage in the UK followed by a long weekend at a European capital city.

◆ Check out the local climate of your destination at the time of year you wish to travel. It is probably wise to avoid certain destinations during hurricane season.

MUSIC FOR THE CEREMONY AND THE RECEPTION

MUSIC FOR THE WEDDING CEREMONY

Music can play an important part in your wedding ceremony. It is another area which you may want to put some careful thought into as the right music can help to create a magical atmosphere.

The type of music you are able to have at your wedding ceremony may be restricted depending upon where you get married.

If you are having a church wedding, hymns and music with religious words are obviously appropriate. Some churches may also allow secular music. You will need to discuss your requirements with the vicar prior to the ceremony to ensure that your choices of music are acceptable and approved.

If you are having a civil ceremony in a hotel or other licensed premises, any music you have must not have any religious content. Again, you will need to discuss your requirements with the registrar beforehand to ensure your choices are acceptable and are approved.

If you are having a register office wedding, you may not be allowed any music at all. You would need to discuss your requirements with the registrar to see if music is allowed at all, but again, this cannot have any religious content.

When searching for appropriate music for your ceremony, you may want to think about the sort of mood you would like to create at various points during the ceremony. You may require pieces of music for:

❖ *The entrance of the Bride*
❖ *The signing of the register*
❖ *The exit (something joyful!)*

❖ Hymns – for church weddings only

It is now possible to get compilation CDs of popular music for wedding ceremonies which could give you some ideas. The internet is another good source of ideas. For civil ceremonies, you may also want to consider songs from films or love songs which have special meaning.

Questions for the Bride and Groom

Have you discussed with the appropriate person whether you are allowed music at your wedding ceremony?

What sort of musicians do you require at the wedding service?

Solo singer	☐
Choir	☐
Harpist	☐
String quartet	☐
Organist	☐
Other _____	☐
None	☐

Do you have a short list of suggestions for

The entrance of the Bride   _____

The singing of the register   _____

The exit   _____

_____

Hymns   _____

_____

Other   _____

_____

Would the music be performed live or would you use a CD?

Does the venue have the facilities to be able to arrange what
you require?

 e.g. does the church have an organ/organist? Does the
 church/venue have a CD player? Are there adequate power
 sockets for any electrical instruments and are there any health
 & safety regulations to comply with?

Music for the Drinks Reception/Sit-down Dinner

You may also decide to have some background music during your drinks reception (if you have one) which could also carry on during a sit-down meal. Background music during these stages of your wedding day can create a relaxed atmosphere as long as it's not too loud so that it stops conversation between your guests.

Questions for the Bride and Groom

Do you require background music
during the drinks reception?

If yes, what type of music?

Harpist	☐
String quartet	☐
CD	☐
Other _____	☐

Have you discussed with the Venue Manager
whether what you are proposing is allowable?

Does the venue have the facilities to be able to arrange
what you require? For example, does the venue have a CD
player/loudspeakers? Are there adequate power sockets for any

electrical instruments and are there any health & safety regulations to comply with?

What type/style of music would you like to have?

Are there any particular pieces of music/songs?

Do you require background music during the sit-down reception? If yes, what type of music?

Harpist	☐
String quartet	☐
CD	☐
Other _____	☐

Have you discussed with the Venue Manager whether what you are proposing is allowable?

Does the venue have the facilities to be able to arrange what you require? For example, does the venue have a CD player/loudspeakers? Are there adequate power sockets for any electrical instruments and are there any health & safety regulations to comply with?

What type/style of music would you like to have?

Are there any particular pieces of music/songs?

EVENING ENTERTAINMENT

Finally, once all the formalities of the day are out of the way, many couples opt for a party/disco in the evening to continue the celebrations well into the night.

This could take the form of live entertainment or a band to get everyone up onto the dance floor.

Questions for the Bride and Groom

What type of entertainment would you like for the evening reception?	DJ/Disco	☐
	Live Band	☐
	Other _____	☐

Have you discussed with the Venue Manager whether what you are proposing is allowable?

Does the venue have the facilities to be able to arrange what you require? For example, does the venue have a CD player/ loudspeakers? Are there adequate power sockets for any electrical instruments and are there any health & safety regulations to comply with?

Do you want to have:

A first dance   Yes ☐

Song title/artist:

_____

A last dance   Yes ☐

Song title/artist:

_____

What type/style of music would
you like at your evening reception:

How would you like the entertainment to be
structured during the evening reception?

Break for buffet?

Background music only during early evening?

THE FIRST DANCE

When considering your first dance, you will need to think about various things, not just the song you choose:

❖ *Does the song have special meaning?*
❖ *Are you able to dance to the song easily?*
❖ *Would it be better to choose something faster/slower?*
❖ *Will your guests be familiar with the song? (You may decide this is not important but if you want them to join you towards the end of the song, you may need to think of a song that people will know and can easily dance to.)*
❖ *How are you going to dance to the song? (If you are not used to dancing together, you may want to practise a few times at home so you are comfortable.)*

There has been a recent trend for engaged couples to go to dance classes and even choreograph scenes from films and music videos for their first dance. There are a number of videos on the internet showing examples of this.

It is possible to book dance lessons through dance companies that can be sourced on the internet and in local directories but in order to accomplish a complicated dance routine, it may be necessary to commit to dedicating a large number of hours to practise enough before the wedding day. It all depends on how much experience in dancing the couple has.

You would need to decide whether it would be feasible for you to take dance classes at the same time as organising everything else. On the other hand, it could be an enjoyable activity, a form of exercise and something that you do together before the wedding.

Questions for the Musicians/DJ

As with all the other suppliers, your search for the right musicians/DJ needs to start with an information gathering exercise to see what is available in your area.

What is the charging structure for the entertainment?
(Deposit/Instalments/Final Payment)

If we want you to play for longer on the day,
are you willing to do this?
If so, what would be the extra fee for this?

Can we come and see you play/sing
at a function?   Yes ☐   No ☐

What type of music do you sing/play?

For live performers only
Do you have a CD of any of your performances?   Yes ☐   No ☐

Can you accommodate our special requests?   Yes ☐   No ☐
  Requests: _____   _____
            _____   _____
            _____   _____

When will you..?
  Arrive   _____

  Leave   _____

Will you require breaks?   Yes ☐   No ☐
   If so, how long?   _____

Will you require food/refreshments?   Yes ☐   No ☐

Have you played at this venue before?   Yes ☐   No ☐

For the DJ and Disco only
Is your equipment PAT (Portable
Appliance Tested) on a yearly basis?   Yes ☐   No ☐

Can we see a copy of your PAT certificate?   Yes ☐   No ☐

Do you bring back-up equipment with you?   Yes ☐   No ☐

What back up plans do you have in place
if something goes wrong beyond your control?

Always inform the venue of the type of entertainment you are
hoping to have and any requirements the performer may have
(e.g. electric sockets for equipment) to ensure what you are
proposing to do is allowable at the venue and complies with all
licensing and insurance regulations.

CHAPTER 13

TASK LISTS

TASK LIST FOR PLANNING YOUR WEDDING DAY

The following is a task list to help you plan your wedding day and to help you think about all the things you will need to arrange.

The timescale is intended to be a guideline only. It will depend on the size of your wedding reception and how complicated your arrangements are as to how far in advance you will need to plan.

The list may also need additional items adding to it depending upon what you decide to book.

The lists are shown in two ways. The first set of lists group tasks by how long there is to go before the wedding day. The second way is a table showing all the tasks for each stage alongside each other.

12 – 18 MONTHS BEFORE YOUR WEDDING DAY

☐ Set a budget for your wedding
☐ Decide on how you are going to finance your wedding
☐ Speak to any family members who are going to help with finance to confirm what they are going to pay for and what amount they can pay
☐ Open a wedding bank account
☐ Set a wedding date, or preferred time of the year – even if provisional
☐ Arrange wedding insurance
☐ Check information on legal marriage by going to your local council website, calling your local Registry Office or speak to your vicar
☐ Choose your best man, ushers, bridesmaids/page boys
☐ Compile Bride and Groom invitation list with both families
☐ Start looking for information on reception venues
☐ Shortlist the venues that meet your requirements
☐ Call reception venues and book appointments to view
☐ Visit reception venues
☐ Provisionally book your selected reception venue
(Do not confirm until ceremony is booked)
☐ If required, search for caterer for venue
☐ Start searching for photographers

☐ Contact photographers for brochures/price lists
☐ Start searching for videographers
☐ Contact videographers for brochures/price lists
☐ Start searching for chauffeurs/transport
☐ Contact chauffeurs for brochures/price lists.

10 – 12 MONTHS BEFORE YOUR WEDDING DAY

- ☐ Book your leave from work
- ☐ Choose location of ceremony
- ☐ Book the church, register office, synagogue or licensed venue.
- ☐ Personnel dealing will the booking will advise you on legal requirements etc
- ☐ If you are provisionally booking a registrar, make a note in your task list to confirm the booking three months prior to the wedding day
- ☐ Provisionally book a date for the wedding rehearsal, if you are getting married in a church
- ☐ Inform all main people required at rehearsal of date
- ☐ Let close family members and friends know the wedding date
- ☐ Once date of ceremony is confirmed, confirm the reception venue booking
- ☐ Pay deposit for reception venue
  (Make a note of when later instalments are due as well as the final payment)
- ☐ Discuss menu options with the reception venue/caterer
- ☐ Book catering
  (If caterers are external to the venue pay deposit and make a note of when later instalments are due as well as the final payment)
- ☐ Shortlist a few photographers
- ☐ Meet with the short listed photographers to discuss requirements

- ☐ Decide on photographer and check they are available
- ☐ Book photographer for the day
  (Pay deposit (if necessary) and make a note of when further instalments and final payment is due)
- ☐ Shortlist a few videographers
- ☐ Meet with the short listed videographers to discuss requirements
- ☐ Decide on videographer and check they are available
- ☐ Book videographer for the day
  (Pay deposit (if necessary) and make a note of when further instalments and final payment is due).

8 – 10 MONTHS BEFORE YOUR WEDDING DAY

- [ ] Nominate two witnesses
- [ ] Look at cake design options
- [ ] Get quotes for cakes
- [ ] Decide on place to get cake from
- [ ] Place the order for the cake
- [ ] Think about wedding dress styles (look at magazines etc)
- [ ] Book appointment to go and try dresses on
- [ ] Decide on final design of dress and where you are getting dress from
- [ ] Order dress
- [ ] Order accessories such as wraps, veils through bridal shop
- [ ] Think about Bridesmaids' dresses
- [ ] Decide on final design of Bridesmaid dresses and where you are getting dress from
- [ ] Order Bridesmaids' dresses
- [ ] Find beautician and hairdresser you trust
- [ ] Consult with beautician and hairdresser regarding your dress style
- [ ] Book for hair and make-up trial one month before wedding day and also for wedding day
- [ ] Select a gift list

- ☐ Review information on wedding cars
- ☐ Meet with a few wedding car companies
- ☐ Decide on type of car
- ☐ Book car for the wedding day
  (Pay deposit and make a note of when instalments and final payment is due)
- ☐ Discuss honeymoon plans
- ☐ Make sure your passports will still be valid up to the date you're due to return
- ☐ Check information on changing the Bride's name on her passport
- ☐ Book your honeymoon.

6 – 8 MONTHS BEFORE YOUR WEDDING DAY

- ☐ Contact reception venue to make sure everything is ok with your booking
- ☐ Contact caterers to make sure everything is ok with your booking
- ☐ Select men's formal wear
  (If hiring formal menswear, choose your preferred style and book the sizes you'll need)
- ☐ Choose and order your wedding rings
- ☐ Find inspiration for your wedding theme
- ☐ Collect some ideas for different wedding invitations and other items e.g. name cards, order of service
- ☐ Obtain quotes for invitations/Work out costs for producing them yourself
- ☐ Decide on design of invitations and other items e.g. name cards, order of service
- ☐ Decide on wording inside your invitations and the other information you want to include
- ☐ Order invitations/Make invitations and other items
- ☐ Decide on wording for Order of Ceremony, menu cards etc
- ☐ Order/Make Order of Ceremony, menu cards etc
- ☐ Arrange date to collect the invitations from the printers or arrange for them to be sent to you
- ☐ Find out if staff at the venue can decorate it for you, or if you can do it yourself

☐ Look at different options for flowers

☐ Book appointment with florist to discuss type of flowers

☐ Agree on flowers and book with florist
(Pay deposit and make a note of when instalments and final payment is due)

☐ Contact photographer to make sure everything is ok with your booking

☐ Contact videographer to make sure everything is ok with your booking

☐ Contact chauffeur to make sure everything is ok with your booking

☐ Consider your Honeymoon requirements, vaccinations, visas, insurance

☐ Decide on type of music/entertainment you would like for the Ceremony/Drinks Reception/Sit down meal/Evening

☐ Contact a few entertainment providers to collect information and prices

☐ Find out facilities for music at the ceremony and reception venues e.g. loudspeakers

☐ Inform ceremony venue/reception venue of your plans for entertainment to ensure it is allowable

☐ Book entertainment
(Pay deposit and make a note of when instalments and final payment is due).

5 MONTHS BEFORE YOUR WEDDING DAY

- ☐ Finalise guest list
- ☐ Arrange accommodation for your wedding night
- ☐ Arrange for dress fitting
- ☐ Buy wedding day lingerie
- ☐ Decide on budget and activities for stag night
- ☐ Send letters telling people the proposed stag date, cost etc
- ☐ Make any necessary provisional stag related bookings (hotel/activities)
- ☐ Decide on budget and activities for hen night
- ☐ Send letters telling people the proposed hen date, cost etc
- ☐ Make any necessary provisional hen related bookings (hotel/activities).

4 MONTHS BEFORE YOUR WEDDING DAY

- ☐ Consult with mothers regarding their outfits
- ☐ Fill in invitations and send them to your guests
- ☐ Send a letter to all confirmed stags to give further details
- ☐ Confirm any stag related bookings (hotel/activities)
- ☐ Send a letter to all confirmed hens to give further details
- ☐ Confirm any hen related bookings (hotel/activities).

3 MONTHS BEFORE YOUR WEDDING DAY

- ☐ Look at changing your name/address on your bank account, credit cards, driver's licence, social security and utilities – seek advice from these organisations on when and how this should be done
- ☐ Discuss your ceremony requirements with your vicar or priest, decide upon church bells, a choir, church flowers, confetti
- ☐ Confirm booking for registrar and ensure all formalities/paperwork is in order
- ☐ Have you sorted out all the legal requirements for the wedding?
- ☐ Confirm rehearsal date
- ☐ Check with main people that they are still available for wedding rehearsal
- ☐ List acceptances and refusals to invitations as they arrive
- ☐ Check reception venue / caterers are still booked for correct date
- ☐ Order table wine and champagne for the toast (either through venue or through caterers or organise this yourselves if allowed to bring alcohol into venue)
- ☐ Check cake is still booked
- ☐ Choose wedding accessories, jewellery, shoes
- ☐ Check florist is still booked for correct date
- ☐ Check photographer is still booked for correct date
- ☐ Check videographer is still booked for correct date

- ☐ Check chauffeur is still booked for correct date
- ☐ Take another look at your passport – check everything is in order
- ☐ Check entertainment still booked for correct date.

2 MONTHS BEFORE YOUR WEDDING DAY

☐ Phone all potential guests that haven't replied to see if they can come
☐ Arrange for fitting of dress
☐ Arrange for fitting of Bridesmaids' dresses
☐ Decide on type of decorations you want
☐ Buy decorations (and confirm with friends/family regarding decorating the venue) or book company to decorate venue
☐ Meet with the photographer to discuss photographs you want taking
☐ Select gifts for the wedding party
☐ Purchase gifts for the wedding party.

1 MONTH BEFORE YOUR WEDDING DAY

- ☐ Write down special readings and give to minister/registrar
- ☐ Confirm time and date of rehearsal with members of your wedding party
- ☐ Inform reception venue/caterers of final numbers and of any special dietary requirements for guests
- ☐ Arrange a reception seating plan
- ☐ Pay final instalment for the venue hire/food/drinks
- ☐ Pay final instalment for the cake
- ☐ Arrange for final fitting of your wedding dress
- ☐ Arrange for final fitting of Bridesmaids' dresses
- ☐ Wear wedding shoes around the house to break them in
- ☐ Get all your holiday clothes together and buy items you need
- ☐ Pack bag of Bride's essentials
- ☐ Check on dresses, suits etc. Is everything going to plan?
- ☐ Collect your wedding rings
- ☐ Trial run of hair and make up and confirm booking for wedding day
- ☐ Write names on place cards
- ☐ Create seating plan for display
- ☐ Pay for the flowers
- ☐ Ensure florist has details of the different locations various flower arrangements need to be delivered to and the times
- ☐ Confirm with family/friends who will help you decorate venue (or speak to person you have booked to do this)

☐ Pay final instalment to the photographer (this might be after the wedding)

☐ Pay final instalment to the videographer (this might be after the wedding)

☐ Pay final instalment for the transport

☐ Write the Groom's speech

☐ Check Best Man has written his speech

☐ Check Father of the Bride has written his speech

☐ Arrange foreign currency/travellers' cheques for your honeymoon

☐ Hold hen and stag nights.

2 WEEKS BEFORE YOUR WEDDING DAY

- ☐ Confirm wedding night accommodation
- ☐ Confirmation with reception venue/caterers
- ☐ Start honeymoon packing
- ☐ Confirmation with florist
- ☐ Confirmation with photographer
- ☐ Confirmation with videographer
- ☐ Confirmation with chauffeur
- ☐ Confirmation with any other supplier you have booked
- ☐ Book taxi or arrange lift to the hotel after the reception/or to airport
- ☐ Work out travel arrangements for all wedding party members and close family and inform them
- ☐ Confirmation with entertainment.

1 WEEK BEFORE YOUR WEDDING DAY

- ☐ Hold wedding rehearsal
- ☐ Final confirmation with hair stylist and make-up person
- ☐ Pack honeymoon suitcase
- ☐ Box up all the decorations and label to take to the venue
- ☐ Collect foreign currency/travellers' cheques.

THE LAST FEW DAYS LEADING UP TO YOUR WEDDING

- ☐ Final confirmation with reception venue/caterers
- ☐ Give venue your wedding planner document with full details
- ☐ Organise to collect the cake
- ☐ Organise for hired clothes to be returned while you are on holiday
- ☐ Have last try of wedding dress
- ☐ Collect wedding dress
- ☐ Collect Bridesmaids' dresses
- ☐ Give Bride's essentials bag to the person responsible for it on the wedding day
- ☐ Final confirmation with florist
- ☐ Final confirmation with photographer
- ☐ Final confirmation with videographer
- ☐ Final confirmation with chauffeur
- ☐ Final confirmation with any other supplier you have booked
- ☐ Final confirmation with friends/family carrying out tasks on wedding day
- ☐ Give written instructions to all members of the wedding party as well as a verbal briefing
- ☐ Give contact numbers of all suppliers to a trustworthy member of your family/friend who can call them on the day if anything doesn't go to plan

- ☐ Give contact number of a trustworthy member of your family/friend to all suppliers so they have a point of contact in case of a problem
- ☐ Final confirmation with entertainment
- ☐ Inform the band/DJ of your first dance song
- ☐ Make final payment to entertainers (if necessary).

THE DAY BEFORE YOUR WEDDING

- ☐ Deliver cake to the reception venue (or arrange for someone to deliver it for you)
- ☐ Ensure the person assembling the cake has adequate instructions
- ☐ Pick up outfits if hiring them
- ☐ Give rings to the best man
- ☐ Arrange for honeymoon/going away clothes to be put in the boot of your car or at your wedding night hotel
- ☐ Decorate Ceremony Venue and Reception Venue
- ☐ Speak to all attendants
- ☐ Give your passports, travel tickets and money to friend or family member
- ☐ Relax and have an early night and set your alarm clock.

	Practical Items	**Ceremony Venue**	**Reception Venue/ Catering/ Cake**
12-18 months	• Set a budget for your wedding • Decide on how you are going to finance your wedding • Speak to family members who are going to help finance • Open a wedding bank account • Set a provisional wedding date • Arrange wedding insurance	• Check information on legal marriage • Choose your best man, ushers, bridesmaids, page boys	• Compile invitation list • Look for information on reception venues • Shortlist reception venues • Book appointments and visit reception venues • Provisionally book selected reception venue • Search for caterers (if required)
10-12 months	• Book your leave from work	• Choose location of ceremony • Book church, register office or other (make note to confirm 3 months before wedding date) • Provisional book rehearsal date • Inform all main people of rehearsal date • Inform close friends and family of wedding date	• Once date of ceremony is confirmed, confirm reception venue booking • Pay deposit for reception venue • Discuss menu options with reception venue or caterer • Book catering

Clothing / Jewellery	Stationery / Decorations	Other Items	Music /
		◆ Start searching for photographers ◆ Contact photographers for brochures/prices ◆ Start searching for videographers ◆ Contact videographers for brochures/prices ◆ Start searching for transport ◆ Contact chauffeurs for brochures/prices	
		◆ Shortlist a few photographers ◆ Meet with short-listed photographers to discuss requirements ◆ Decide on photographer and book ◆ Shortlist a few videographers ◆ Meet with short-listed videographers to discuss requirements ◆ Decide on videographer and book	

	Practical Items	Ceremony Venue	Reception Venue/ Catering/ Cake
8-10 months		◆ Nominate two witnesses	◆ Look at cake design options ◆ Get quotes for cakes ◆ Decide on place to get cake from ◆ Place the order for the cake

Clothing / Jewellery	Stationery / Decorations	Other Items	Music / Entertainment
◆ Think about wedding dress styles ◆ Book appointment to try on dresses ◆ Decide on final design and where you are getting the dress from ◆ Order dress ◆ Order accessories such as wraps, veils through bridal shop ◆ Think about Bridesmaids' dresses ◆ Decide on final design and where you are getting the Bridesmaids' dresses from ◆ Order Bridesmaids' dresses ◆ Find beautician and hairdresser you trust ◆ Consult with beautician and hairdresser regarding dress style ◆ Book hair and make-up trial for one month before your wedding day and for your wedding day	◆ Select a gift list	◆ Review information on wedding cars ◆ Meet with a few wedding car companies ◆ Decide on type of car ◆ Book car for wedding day ◆ Discuss honeymoon plans ◆ Make sure passports are valid up to date of return ◆ Check information about changing Bride's name on passport ◆ Book your honeymoon	

	Practical Items	Ceremony Venue	Reception Venue/ Catering/ Cake
6-8 months			◆ Contact reception venue to make sure everything is ok ◆ Contact caterers to make sure everything is ok

Clothing / Jewellery	Stationery / Decorations	Other Items	Music / Entertainment
◆ Select men's formal wear (If hiring choose style, book sizes required) ◆ Choose and order wedding rings	◆ Find inspiration for your wedding theme ◆ Collect some ideas for invitations etc ◆ Obtain quotes for invitations/work out costs of producing them yourself ◆ Decide on design for invitations and other stationery ◆ Decide on wording for invitations and other information to include ◆ Order/make invitations ◆ Decide on wording for other items ◆ Order/make other items ◆ Arrange a date to collect invitations etc from printers ◆ Find out if venue staff can decorate it ◆ Look at options for flowers ◆ Book appointment with florist ◆ Agree on flowers and book with florist	◆ Contact photographer to make sure everything is ok ◆ Contact videographer to make sure everything is ok ◆ Contact chauffeur to make sure everything is ok ◆ Consider your honeymoon requirements, vaccinations, visas, insurance	◆ Decide on type of music for ceremony/drinks reception/meal/ evening ◆ Contact entertainment providers for prices ◆ Find out facilities at ceremony and reception venues for music ◆ Inform ceremony and reception venues of your plans for music to ensure it is allowable ◆ Book entertainment

	Practical Items	Ceremony Venue	Reception Venue/ Catering/ Cake
5 months			◆ Finalise guest list ◆ Arrange accommodation for your wedding night
4 months			

Clothing / Jewellery	Stationery / Decorations	Other Items	Music / Entertainment
◆ Arrange dress fitting ◆ Buy wedding day lingerie		◆ Decide on budget and activities for stag night ◆ Send letters telling people proposed stag date, cost etc ◆ Make any necessary provisional stag related bookings (hotel, activities) ◆ Decide on budget and activities for hen night ◆ Send letters telling people proposed hen date, cost etc ◆ Make any necessary provisional hen related bookings (hotel, activities)	
◆ Consult with mothers regarding outfits	◆ Fill in invitations and send them to guests	◆ Send a letter to all confirmed stags giving further details ◆ Confirm any stag related activities (hotel, activities) ◆ Send a letter to all confirmed hens giving further details ◆ Confirm any hens related activities (hotel, activities)	

	Practical Items	Ceremony Venue	Reception Venue/ Catering/ Cake
3 months	◆ Look at changing the Bride's name on bank account, utilities etc – seek advice from all organisations	◆ Discuss your ceremony requirements with vicar ◆ Confirm booking for registrar and ensure all formalities are in order ◆ Confirm rehearsal date ◆ Check main people are still available for the rehearsal	◆ List acceptances and refusals to invitations as they arrive ◆ Check reception venue and caterer are still booked for correct date ◆ Order drinks for drinks reception, tables and for toast ◆ Check cake is still booked
2 months			◆ Phone all potential guests that haven't replied

Clothing / Jewellery	Stationery / Decorations	Other Items	Music / Entertainment
◆ Choose wedding accessories, jewellery, shoes	◆ Check florist is still booked for correct date	◆ Check photographer is still booked for correct date ◆ Check videographer is still booked for correct date ◆ Check chauffeur is still booked for correct date ◆ Take another look at your passport to check everything is in order	◆ Check entertainment is booked for the correct date
◆ Arrange for fitting of dress ◆ Arrange for fitting of Bridesmaids' dresses	◆ Decide on type of decorations you want ◆ Buy decorations ◆ Confirm with friends and family they can decorate the venue or book company or venue staff to do it	◆ Meet with photographer to discuss photographs ◆ Select gifts for wedding party ◆ Purchase gifts for wedding party	

	Practical Items	Ceremony Venue	Reception Venue/ Catering/ Cake
1 month		◆ Write down special readings and give to minister/ registrar ◆ Confirm date and time of rehearsal with wedding party	◆ Inform reception venue/caterers of final numbers and any special dietary requirements of guests ◆ Arrange reception seating plan ◆ Pay final instalment for venue hire/food/ drinks ◆ Pay final instalment for cake

Clothing / Jewellery	Stationery / Decorations	Other Items	Music / Entertainment
◆ Arrange for final fitting of wedding dress ◆ Arrange for final fitting of Bridesmaids' dresses ◆ Wear wedding shoes around the house to break them in ◆ Get all your holiday clothes together and buy items you need ◆ Pack bag of Bride's essentials ◆ Check on dresses, suits etc – is everything going to plan? ◆ Collect your wedding rings ◆ Trial run of hair and makeup and confirm booking for wedding day	◆ Write names on place cards ◆ Create seating plan for display ◆ Pay for flowers ◆ Ensure florist has details of locations, arrangements to be delivered and delivery times ◆ Confirm with family/friends who will help you decorate venue or speak to person you have booked for this	◆ Pay final instalment to photographer (this might be after the wedding) ◆ Pay final instalment to videographer (this might be after the wedding) ◆ Pay final instalment for transport ◆ Write the Groom's speech ◆ Check Best Man has written his speech ◆ Check Father of the Bride has written his speech ◆ Arrange foreign currency/travellers' cheques for your honeymoon ◆ Hold hen and stag nights	

	Practical Items	Ceremony Venue	Reception Venue/ Catering/ Cake
2 weeks			◆ Confirm wedding night accommodation ◆ Confirmation with reception venue/caterers
1 week		◆ Hold wedding rehearsal	

Clothing / Jewellery	Stationery / Decorations	Other Items	Music / Entertainment
◆ Start honeymoon packing	◆ Confirmation with florist	◆ Confirmation with photographer ◆ Confirmation with videographer ◆ Confirmation with chauffeur ◆ Confirmation with any other supplier you have booked ◆ Book taxi or arrange lift to hotel after the reception or to airport ◆ Work out travel arrangements for all wedding party members and close family and inform them	◆ Confirmation with entertainment
◆ Final confirmation with hair stylist/make-up person ◆ Pack honeymoon suitcase	◆ Box up decorations, label and take to the venue	◆ Collect foreign currency/travellers' cheques	

	Practical Items	Ceremony Venue	Reception Venue/ Catering/ Cake
Last few days			◆ Final confirmation with venue/ caterers ◆ Give venue your wedding planner document with full details ◆ Organise to collect cake

Clothing / Jewellery	Stationery / Decorations	Other Items	Music / Entertainment
◆ Organise for hired clothes to be returned while you are on holiday ◆ Have last try of dress ◆ Collect wedding dress ◆ Collect Bridesmaids' dresses ◆ Give Bride's essentials bag to person responsible for it on wedding day	◆ Final confirmation with florist	◆ Final confirmation with photographer ◆ Final confirmation with videographer ◆ Final confirmation with chauffeur ◆ Final confirmation with any other supplier you have booked ◆ Final confirmation with friends/family carrying out tasks on the day ◆ Give written instructions to members of wedding party as well as verbal ◆ Give contact numbers of suppliers to trustworthy person ◆ Give contact number of trustworthy person to all suppliers	◆ Final confirmation with entertainment ◆ Inform band/DJ of your first dance song ◆ Make any final payments to entertainers (if necessary)

	Practical Items	**Ceremony Venue**	**Reception Venue/ Catering/ Cake**
Day before			◆ Deliver cake to reception venue ◆ Ensure person assembling cake has instructions

Clothing / Jewellery	Stationery / Decorations	Other Items	Music / Entertainment
◆ Pick up outfits (if hiring them) ◆ Give rings to Best Man ◆ Arrange for honeymoon clothes to be in boot of your car or at wedding night hotel	◆ Decorate ceremony venue/ reception venue	◆ Speak to all attendants ◆ Give your passport, travel tickets and money to family member ◆ Relax, have an early night and set your alarm clock	

INDEX